GLOBALVIEWPOINTS

Child Labor

Other Books of Related Interest:

GLOBALVIEWPOINTS

Child Labor

Gary Wiener, Book Editor

GREENHAVEN PRESS
A part of Gale, Cengage Learning

GALE
CENGAGE Learning·

Detroit • New York • San Francisco • New Haven, Conn • Waterville, Maine • London

GALE
CENGAGE Learning

Christine Nasso, *Publisher*
Elizabeth Des Chenes, *Managing Editor*

© 2009 Greenhaven Press, a part of Gale, Cengage Learning

Gale and Greenhaven Press are registered trademarks used herein under license.

For more information, contact:
Greenhaven Press
27500 Drake Rd.
Farmington Hills, MI 48331-3535
Or you can visit our Internet site at gale.cengage.com

For product information and technology assistance, contact us at

Gale Customer Support, 1-800-877-4253
For permission to use material from this text or product, submit all requests online at www.cengage.com/permissions

Further permissions questions can be emailed to permissionrequest@cengage.com

Articles in Greenhaven Press anthologies are often edited for length to meet page requirements. In addition, original titles of these works are changed to clearly present the main thesis and to explicitly indicate the author's opinion. Every effort is made to ensure that Greenhaven Press accurately reflects the original intent of the authors. Every effort has been made to trace the owners of copyrighted material.

Cover image copyright Paul Prescott, 2009. Used under license from Shutterstock.com.

LIBRARY OF CONGRESS CATALOGING-IN-PUBLICATION DATA

Child labor / Gary Wiener, book editor.
    p. cm. -- (Global viewpoints)
    Includes bibliographical references and index.
    ISBN 978-0-7377-4330-2 (hardcover)
    ISBN 978-0-7377-4329-6 (pbk.)
    1. Child labor. I. Wiener, Gary.
    HD6231.C45 2009
    331.3'1--dc22
                                                              2009005238

Printed in the United States of America
2 3 4 5 6   13 12 11 10 09

ED271

Contents

Chapter 1: The Global Problem of Child Labor

Chapter 2: The Dangers of Child Labor

Chapter 3: Defending Child Labor

Chapter 4: Efforts to End Child Labor Around the World

Foreword

"The problems of all of humanity can only be solved by all of humanity."
—Swiss author Friedrich Dürrenmatt

Global interdependence has become an undeniable reality. Mass media and technology have increased worldwide access to information and created a society of global citizens. Understanding and navigating this global community is a challenge, requiring a high degree of information literacy and a new level of learning sophistication.

Building on the success of its flagship series, *Opposing Viewpoints*, Greenhaven Press has created the *Global Viewpoints* series to examine a broad range of current, often controversial topics of worldwide importance from a variety of international perspectives. Providing students and other readers with the information they need to explore global connections and think critically about worldwide implications, each *Global Viewpoints* volume offers a panoramic view of a topic of widespread significance.

Drugs, famine, immigration—a broad, international treatment is essential to do justice to social, environmental, health, and political issues such as these. Junior high, high school, and early college students, as well as general readers, can all use *Global Viewpoints* anthologies to discern the complexities relating to each issue. Readers will be able to examine unique national perspectives while, at the same time, appreciating the interconnectedness that global priorities bring to all nations and cultures.

Material in each volume is selected from a diverse range of sources, including journals, magazines, newspapers, nonfiction books, speeches, government documents, pamphlets, organization newsletters, and position papers. *Global Viewpoints* is truly global, with material drawn primarily from international sources available in English and secondarily from U.S. sources with extensive international coverage.

Features of each volume in the *Global Viewpoints* series include:

- An **annotated table of contents** that provides a brief summary of each essay in the volume, including the name of the country or area covered in the essay.

- An **introduction** specific to the volume topic.

- A **world map** to help readers locate the countries or areas covered in the essays.

- For each viewpoint, an **introduction** that contains notes about the author and source of the viewpoint explains why material from the specific country is being presented, summarizes the main points of the viewpoint, and offers three **guided reading questions** to aid in understanding and comprehension.

- **For further discussion** questions that promote critical thinking by asking the reader to compare and contrast aspects of the viewpoints or draw conclusions about perspectives and arguments.

- A worldwide list of **organizations to contact** for readers seeking additional information.

- A **periodical bibliography** for each chapter and a **bibliography of books** on the volume topic to aid in further research.

- A comprehensive **subject index** to offer access to people, places, events, and subjects cited in the text, with the countries covered in the viewpoints highlighted.

Global Viewpoints is designed for a broad spectrum of readers who want to learn more about current events, history, political science, government, international relations, economics, environmental science, world cultures, and sociology—students doing research for class assignments or debates, teachers and faculty seeking to supplement course materials, and others wanting to understand current issues better. By presenting how people in various countries perceive the root causes, current consequences, and proposed solutions to worldwide challenges, *Global Viewpoints* volumes offer readers opportunities to enhance their global awareness and their knowledge of cultures worldwide.

Introduction

> "Child labor and poverty are inevitably bound together and if you continue to use the labor of children as the treatment for the social disease of poverty, you will have both poverty and child labor to the end of time."
>
> —Grace Abbott,
> director, Children's Bureau,
> U.S. Department of Labor, 1917–1934

When most people think of child labor, they may either conjure up Dickensian nightmares of nineteenth-century pre-adolescent chimney sweeps and factory workers, or far away visions of children in third world countries laboring in sweatshops or under a broiling equatorial sun. While the latter scenarios are certainly still current in our globalized world, child labor is a problem *everywhere* in the twenty-first century, with an estimated 250 million children from ages five to fourteen still laboring in developed, as well as in third world, nations. Child labor is as commonly found among immigrant migrant workers in rural Alabama as it is in the slums of Mumbai, India. As Columbia University professor Jagdish Bhagwati writes, "even a country as rich as the United States still has children at work, not just selling lemonade and cookies on the roadside or hosing down your car for a buck, but in the poor counties in the South where migrant labor works under exploitive conditions."

When discussing child labor, it is important to begin with a definition of terms. One must distinguish especially between "child work" and "child labor." Few people have a problem with a 14-year-old working on the family farm doing chores from three o'clock in the afternoon to five o'clock after school every day. Almost no one would complain about 12-year-olds delivering newspapers at six in the morning six days a week. We mostly file such entrepreneurial enterprises under the category of child work and admire youngsters who display the drive and determination to help their families or better themselves at an early age. But such occupations are a far cry from those of child soldiers, forced into combat in the Democratic Republic of the Congo, or pre-teens in the slums of Pakistan who labor fourteen hours or more a day, their small fingers knotting Indian rugs in sweatshop conditions for upscale consumers in, say, Evanston, Illinois, or Hamburg, Germany. These are examples of child labor in its worst forms, and most free-thinking, open-minded citizens of any country would object to such harsh forms of employment.

In one form or another child labor has existed since there have been children. Our contemporary conception of childhood as a sacred time of innocence and play is actually a fairly new phenomenon, historically speaking, with roots in the nineteenth century. The same can be said of our modern notion of motherhood. In the words of Nobel laureate Toni Morrison, "The idea of motherhood—of the ideal mother—caring . . . for her child, is really a relatively modern notion. . . . Mothers were breeders, and people had lots of children because they needed their labor, and you could just as easily abandon the child as keep it."

In ancient times, up until the Industrial Revolution, child labor usually took the form of agricultural laborers who often toiled on a family or communal farm. Their labors usually occurred far enough from population centers so as to remain away from the scrutiny of those who might condemn it. Even many well-intentioned observers who came across children toiling in the fields might have mistaken such hardship for a character-building enterprise. When English novelist Daniel Defoe, author of *Robinson Crusoe* and a firm believer in the value of hard work, toured the eastern counties of England in

1723, he was very much impressed to find no "hand unemployed, if they would work; and that the very children, after four or five years of age, could every one earn their own bread" by working in the cotton fields.

With the flight to cities that occurred upon the advent of industrialism in the late-eighteenth and nineteenth centuries, children were used to fill the increasing need for a cheap labor force. Factory work was most often long, laborious, and financially unrewarding, so much so that in 1819 the romantic poet Samuel Taylor Coleridge characterized the children as "our poor little white slaves." Though many modern Englishmen still saw absolutely nothing wrong with subjecting poverty-stricken young people to arduous labor, in the nineteenth century a succession of British "factory laws" were passed, aimed at curtailing the long hours and prohibiting children from working before they were nine years old. But progress was slow in Britain. Not until 1937 did a subsequent Factories Act raise the working age to twelve. Child labor died equally as hard in the United States, where the first truly effective law curtailing child labor, the First Labor Standards Act, was not enacted until 1938. This law mandated a minimum age of eighteen for those engaged in activities that were deemed hazardous and prohibited those under sixteen from working during school hours. Many scholars believe that it was not such laws alone that ended the widespread practice of child labor, and instead credit this development to changing economic conditions and, especially, compulsory education.

But even as the industrialized nations were finally taking steps to end child labor, the third world juvenile labor force came under increasing scrutiny. Because many governments struggled to fight child labor, in the twentieth century the cause was taken up by myriad NGOs, or non-governmental organizations. Today, the fight against child labor is just as likely to be led by Human Rights Watch or the United Nations Children's Fund (UNICEF) as by the U.S. Department of Labor. Twenty-first century child labor is so ingrained and extensive that no one organization or government can seemingly make a dent. Thus, there are literally hundreds of organizations around the world dedicated to attacking the child labor problem, from the multi-national Rugmark, which seeks to eliminate child labor in the rug and carpet industry by certifying that carpets are not produced by young people, to Free the Children, a Toronto, Canada-based NGO that combats child labor by empowering children around the globe. In particular, the International Labour Organization (ILO) based in Geneva, Switzerland, and operating under the auspices of the United Nations, has been an effective and tireless advocate for the rights of children through its International Programme on the Elimination of Child Labour (IPEC).

Several important international "conventions," designed to tackle child labor on a global scale, were initiated in the late twentieth century. Included among these is the United Nations Convention on the Rights of the Child, often referred to as CRC or UNCRC. This 1989 convention is an international agreement that delineates the civil, political, economic, social, and cultural rights of children. Nations that voluntarily ratify this international convention are bound by international law to uphold human rights for children in their countries. In 1999 the ILO adopted what has become known as Convention 182, "The Convention Concerning the Prohibition and Immediate Action for the Elimination of the Worst Forms of Child Labour," known in short as the Worst Forms of Child Labour Convention. This convention focuses on such egregious exploitation of children as child slavery, child sex trafficking, and child soldiering. This focus on the worst forms of child labor has ensured exceptional results, with 162 countries having signed on to abide by the convention as of June 2007.

In spite of these and other advances in world attitudes toward child labor, twenty-first century globalization has fueled the need for child workers to produce goods for exportation and has given rise to an ongoing debate as to the reasons for child labor and the best ways to eliminate it. One central question is whether poverty fuels child labor or child labor continues the cycle of poverty. Conservatives and so-called neo-liberals, including free-market capitalists and defenders of globalization, believe that child labor is an inevitable outgrowth of poverty, and that outlawing child labor, however well-intentioned, at best will fail to alleviate the root problem and at worst will cause even more problems. In his encyclopedic study entitled *Capitalism*, Pepperdine University professor George Reisman writes, "The abolition or reduction of child labor by law, rather than by the voluntary decisions of parents in a progressing economy, ignore the precondition of the productivity of labor being high enough to enable the parents to afford its reduction or abolition. As a result, child labor laws have had the perverse effect of rendering poor families still poorer, and, in so doing, of jeopardizing the health and well-being of the very children they were intended to protect." Jagdish Bhagwati adds that laws prohibiting child labor "will only drive poor parents to send their children to work by stealth and often into even worse 'occupations' such as prostitution." He observes that "This happened in Bangladesh, with some young girls falling into prostitution when garment employers who feared the passage of the U.S. Child Labor Deterrence Act," laid off as many as fifty thousand young factory workers. Thus conservatives hold that child work helps poor families meet the bottom line and is a way out of poverty for third world nations.

Many liberals, and those who view child labor as inherently exploitative and evil, argue that contrary to the conservative view, child labor only perpetuates the cycle of poverty. Child labor, they believe, prevents children from being where they should be at a young age: in school. Children who work long hours either get an inferior education, or none at all, and grow up without the necessary skills and education that will make them viable and productive members of the workforce. As Massachusetts Institute of Technology professor Lester Thurow writes, "Child labor did not slowly die out in the United States as Americans grew richer. At some point Americans woke up and made it illegal. Ending child labor is in the self-interest of any country. . . . Child labor is not going to lead anyone into the promised land of economic development. More important, it is simply morally wrong. In every country, no matter how poor, forcing young children to work outside of the home is abusive exploitation."

Global Viewpoints: Child Labor examines current issues surrounding the ongoing controversy concerning the use of children in the work environment in countries from Brazil to Pakistan. The authors included in this volume attempt to define child labor and to investigate its worst forms—including child soldiers and prostitutes—around the world. Authors also argue the pros and cons of a free market, laissez-faire attitude toward child labor versus the attempt to impose strict sanctions against those who profit from child work. Finally, authors in the book's last section describe worldwide efforts to bring this practice to an end.

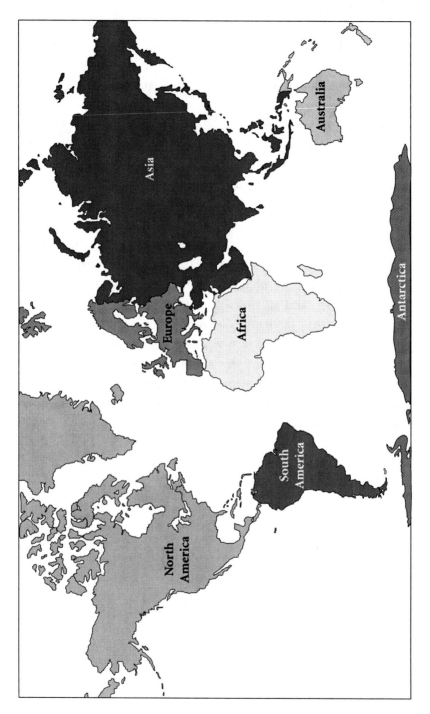

 **GLOBAL**VIEWPOINTS

CHAPTER 1

The Global Problem of Child Labor

Child Labor Defined

Chivy Sok

In the following viewpoint, Chivy Sok asserts that child labor is a complex term with no single definition. Human rights organizations generally agree that child labor is work that may interfere with a child's education, or may be harmful to the child's body or mind. Child labor is prevalent throughout the world, though it is most pervasive in the Asia-Pacific region. Most people think of child labor as a problem only in developing nations, but it occurs frequently even in developed nations like the United States. Chivy Sok has served as the deputy director of the University of Iowa Center for Human Rights (UICHR) and as project director of the University's Child Labor Research Initiative (CLRI). She advocates for international human rights and works for the advancement of peace and social justice.

As you read, consider the following questions:

1. How did the 1989 United Nations Convention on the Rights of the Child define child labor?
2. What four categories constitute the worst forms of child labor?
3. According to Sok, where is child labor found in America?

About 246 million children between the ages of 5 and 17 are engaged in "child labor," according to the International Labour Organization's (ILO) 2000 global estimate. An estimated 73 million of these children are below the age of 10.

What is meant by "child labor"? What kind of work constitutes child labor? And where are these child laborers found? How is child labor connected to us as Americans? These are very simple questions. The answers, unfortunately, are not so simple.

It has taken many years to come to some kind of agreement on the definition of child labor. While experts continue to disagree on some aspects of the definition, two international human-rights conventions have helped to guide international efforts to eliminate child labor.

The first comes from the 1989 UN Convention on the Rights of the Child. According to Article 32 of this convention, "State Parties recognize the right of the child to be protected from economic exploitation and from performing any work that is likely to be hazardous or to interfere with the child's education, or to be harmful to the child's health or physical, mental, spiritual, moral, or social development."

A decade later, the ILO adopted a new convention that further defines the worst forms of child labor, the kind of work that is completely unacceptable and needs to be eliminated as soon as possible. The new ILO convention, commonly referred to as the Worst Forms of Child Labor Convention, defines the worst forms this way:

1. All forms of slavery or practices similar to slavery, such as the sale and trafficking of children, debt bondage and serfdom, and forced or compulsory labor, including forced or compulsory recruitment of children for use in armed conflict;

2. The use, procuring, or offering of a child for prostitution, for the production of pornography, or for pornographic performances;

3. The use, procuring, or offering of a child for illicit activities, in particular for the "production and trafficking of drugs as defined in the relevant international treaties; and

4. Work which, by its nature or the circumstances in which it is carried out, is likely to harm the health, safety, or morals of children. This last category is commonly referred to as "hazardous work."

In 2000, the ILO conducted a study of the scope and magnitude of child labor. The Asia-Pacific region has the highest incidence of child labor. About 127.3 million children between the ages of 5 and 14 are found in Asia, 73 million in sub-Saharan Africa, and 17.4 million in Latin America and the Caribbean. And about 5 million are found in both developed countries and transition economies. This is only an estimate; it is nearly impossible to accurately measure the problem. But we know that this problem is widespread.

When people hear the phrase "child labor," they often think of problems in faraway places—problems in poor, developing countries. While it is true that the highest incidence of child labor takes place in these poor countries, America has its share of the problem. In fact, American history is filled with abusive forms of child labor, such as children working in mines, sawmills, and sweatshop factories. Today, some child labor continues to exist in America. We can still find children working on farms under some of the most hazardous conditions. In states such as California and Texas, for example, children are picking onions and other agricultural products that end up in some of our supermarkets and that are eaten by you and me.

As Americans, we are also connected to global child labor, directly and indirectly. About 70 percent of child labor takes place in agriculture. This includes the harvesting of bananas in Central America and cocoa beans for chocolate in West Africa and the picking of coffee beans and tea leaves in Latin

Defining Child Labor

Not all work done by children should be classified as child labour that is to be targeted for elimination. Children's or adolescents' participation in work that does not affect their health and personal development or interfere with their schooling, is generally regarded as being something positive. This includes activities such as helping their parents around the home, assisting in a family business or earning pocket money outside school hours and during school holidays. . . .

The term "child labour" is often defined as work that deprives children of their childhood, their potential and their dignity, and that is harmful to physical and mental development. It refers to work that:

- is mentally, physically, socially or morally dangerous and harmful to children; and

- interferes with their schooling by depriving them of the opportunity to attend school; by obliging them to leave school prematurely; or by requiring them to attempt to combine school attendance with excessively long and heavy work.

In its most extreme forms, child labour involves children being enslaved, separated from their families, exposed to serious hazards and illnesses and/or left to fend for themselves on the streets of large cities. . . .

Whether or not particular forms of "work" can be called "child labour" depends on the child's age, the type and hours of work performed, the conditions under which it is performed and the objectives pursued by individual countries. The answer varies from country to country, as well as among sectors within countries.

International Labour Office, Child Labour:
A Textbook for University Students, *2004.*

America and Africa. Some of these agricultural products end up on our supermarket shelves. For better or for worse, we are connected to some of the most unacceptable forms of child labor.

American history is filled with abusive forms of child labor, such as children working in mines, sawmills, and sweatshop factories.

Besides agriculture, what other forms of child labor exist? The list is long, and we can only cite a few categories, to give an idea of the scope of the problem. Some children are trafficked for forced labor or put into some of the most degrading kind of work. Some are used to promote illicit activities such as the drug trade. Some children are kidnapped and forced to become child soldiers. Others are abducted to perform labor similar to slavery, such as becoming camel jockeys or working as servants in other people's homes. Other children, especially those orphaned by HIV/AIDS, are left to fend for themselves on the streets. These are the children who labor from dawn until dusk in dangerous conditions and live without knowing where their next meal will come from.

These 246 million children suffer from some of the cruelest human rights violations on a daily basis.

About 70 percent of child labor takes place in agriculture.

Through Time

1639 The earliest recorded account of cruelty to a child occurred when a master killed his young apprentice.

1790s Child labor rose in the United States during the Industrial Revolution. Eventually laws were passed to limit how much children can work.

1904 The National Child Labor Committee was formed in the United States.

1909 The first Conference on Children was held at the White House.

1912 The United States Congress founded the Children's Bureau.

1916 The Keating-Owen Act forbade the sale of any item produced by child labor. The Supreme Court later decided the act was unconstitutional.

1938 The United States Congress passed the Fair Labor Standards Act, freeing children under the age of 16 from having to work.

1974 The United States Congress created the Child Abuse Prevention and Treatment Act.

1989 The United Nations adopted the Convention on the Rights of the Child. The convention asks that all member nations protect their children's rights.

1995 Twelve-year-old Craig Kielburger founded Free the Children, an international organization of children who help other children.

1999 The International Labor Organization adopts the Convention on the Worst Forms of Child Labor.

2000 The Harkin-Engel Protocol is adopted to address child slavery in the chocolate industry. The United Nations adopts the Millennium Development Goals (MDG).

2001 The international global movement Say Yes for Children began to gain millions of members worldwide.

2002 More than 400 child delegates attended the United Nations General Assembly special session on children.

2004 The first Children's World Congress on child labor is held in Florence, Italy. A follow-up session is held in India the following year.

2006 As many as 250 million children are being held in bondage and working as slaves around the world.

Chivy Sok is a human rights advocate and consulting editor of this issue.

Indian Children Make American Goods

Megha Bahree

In the following viewpoint, Megha Bahree writes that despite laws against child labor in India, children as young as five years of age work at jobs that are often hazardous. The products of their labors are seen on store shelves in Europe and North America. There are watchdog groups that oversee production and attempt to guard against child workers, but Indian businessmen and farmers easily circumvent most overseers. All corporations that use Indian workers claim to prohibit child laborers, but according to Bahree, the reality is that many of their products are made by the very workers to whom they say they deny jobs. India has become a sweatshop for the world, Bahree asserts. Megha Bahree is a reporter who has written about India, Afghanistan, and Palestine.

As you read, consider the following questions:

1. According to Bahree why don't American retailers enforce all child labor laws in India?

2. According to cottonseed farmer Talari Babu, why are children better suited to harvesting cotton than adults?

3. What are some of the different solutions to child labor proposed by labor organizations?

Megha Bahree, "Child Labor," *Forbes Global*, vol. 4, no. 4, March 10, 2008, p. 62.

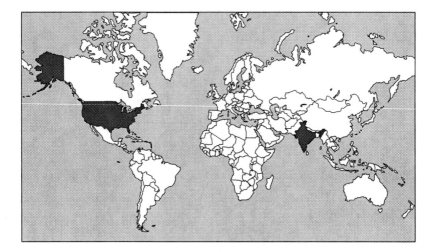

Yothi Ramulla Naga is 4 feet tall. From sunup to sundown she is hunched over in the fields of a cottonseed farm in southern India, earning 20 cents an hour. Farmers in the Uyyalawada region process high-tech cottonseeds genetically engineered to contain a natural pesticide, on behalf of U.S. agriculture giant Monsanto.

To get the seeds to breed true the farmers have to cross-pollinate the plants, a laborious task that keeps a peak of a dozen workers busy for several months on just one acre. And to make a profit the farmers have to use cheap labor. That means using kids like Jyothi, who says she's 15 but looks no older than 12. (Monsanto points to papers indicating she is 15.) To harvest the bolls three months later, the farmers use cheap labor again, not the machinery that is used to pick cotton in the U.S.

At the edge of where Jyothi is working, a rusting sign proclaims, "Monsanto India Limited Child Labour Free Fields." Jyothi says she has been working in these fields for the past five years, since her father, a cotton farmer, committed suicide after incurring huge debts. On a recent December morning there were teens picking cotton in nearly all of a half-dozen Monsanto farms in Uyyalawada, 250 miles south of India's high-tech hub Hyderabad. Last year 420,000 laborers under the age of 18 were employed in cottonseed farms in four states across India, estimates Glocal Research, a consultancy in Hyderabad that monitors agricultural labor conditions. Of that total 54% were under the age of 14 and illegally employed.

Even as India gallops toward First World status . . . it is still a giant backyard sweatshop to the world, staffed by underage boys and girls.

The law prohibits children under 14 from working in factories, slaughterhouses or other dangerous locations. There are some exceptions for farmwork—if the hours are limited, the kids are in school and there are no machines to be operated. But children like Jyothi put in ten-hour days in the field and miss school. Teenagers 14 to 18 years old can work during the day in factories but no more than 36 hours a week. Employer penalties include fines and imprisonment. But enforcement of the law is lax.

Even as India gallops toward First World status—with its booming economy, roaring stock market and rapid progress in autos and steel—it is still a giant backyard sweatshop to the world, staffed by underage boys and girls. The government itself, in its most recent account (from a 2001 census), estimates that 12.6 million children under the age of 14 are at work in India. NGOs that make a career of exposing excesses put the number much higher—50 million.

Child labor is as old as the earliest settlements in the Indus Valley thousands of years ago. It is, for that matter, not unknown in the U.S. As recently as 2001 Nebraska's legislature was debating whether to outlaw the use of 12- and 13-year-olds in seed corn fields, where youngsters of this age accounted for 25% or more of detasseling labor. (This job is like Jyothi's, except that in hybrid seed corn production the game is to prevent self-pollination.) The difference is that the teenagers in the Midwest get $7 an hour so they can spend it at the mall. Their Indian counterparts are getting 20 cents an hour to buy food.

Every time somebody in the U.S. buys an imported handmade carpet, an embroidered pair of jeans, a beaded purse, a decorated box or a soccer ball, there's a good chance they're acquiring something fashioned by a child.

Every time somebody in Europe or the U.S. buys an imported handmade carpet, an embroidered pair of jeans, a beaded purse, a decorated box or a soccer ball, there's a good chance they're acquiring something fashioned by a child. Such goods are available in places like GapKids, Macy's, ABC Carpet & Home, Ikea, Lowe's and Home Depot.

These retailers say they are aware of child-labor problems, have strict policies against selling products made by underage kids and abide by the laws of the countries from which they import. But there are many links in a supply chain, and even a well-intentioned importer can't police them all.

"There are many, many household items that are produced with forced labor and not just child labor," says Bama Athreya, executive director of the International Labor Rights Forum in Washington, D.C. It's a fact of a global economy, and will continue to be, as long as Americans (and Europeans) demand cheap goods—and incomes in emerging economies remain low. If a child is enslaved, it's because his parents are desperately poor.

The UN International Labor Organization guesses that there are 218 million child laborers worldwide, 7 in 10 of them in agriculture, followed by service businesses (22%) and industry (9%). Asia-Pacific claims the greatest share of underage workers (122 million), then sub-Saharan Africa (49 million). Noteworthy offenders: Cambodia, Mali, Bangladesh, Sri Lanka and Guatemala (see chart). A decade ago India ratified the UN convention on children's rights but refused to sign one key clause that set the standard for child labor—14 and under. "This already waters down their obligations under international law, which of course remains a voluntary matter," says Coen Kompier at the ILO's New Delhi bureau.

Cottonseed farmer Talari Babu is a slim, wiry man dressed, when a reporter visited him, in black for a Hindu fast. "Children have small fingers, and so they can remove the buds very quickly," he says, while insisting that he no longer employs the underage. "They worked fast, much faster than the adults, and put in longer hours and didn't demand long breaks. Plus, I could shout at them and beat or threaten them if need be to get more work out of them." He could also tempt them with candy and cookies and movies at night. Babu says that pressure from Monsanto and the MV Foundation, an NGO in Andhra Pradesh backed by the Dutch nonprofit Hivos, forced him to quit using child labor. But minutes after a visitor arrives at his field, he receives a call on his cell phone asking him if a raid was being carried out on his farm. In 2006, he says, Monsanto paid him a $360 bonus for not using child laborers. The bonus, though, doesn't make up for the higher wages that adults command. Says Babu: "Had I used children, I would've earned more."

Monsanto's competitors, the Swiss Syngenta and the German Bayer, also contract with farmers in India to produce seed. For all three the arrangement is like the one that governs chicken production in the U.S., with a giant corporation supplying inputs to a small farmer and then picking up the output at harvest time.

A typical Monsanto farmer owns only 1 to 4 acres of intensely cultivated cotton plants and keeps up to a dozen workers busy for the better part of a year tending to the plot. Often the farmer is from a higher caste (Brahmin), the laborers from a landless lower caste (Dalit). The pay, typically $38 to $76 a month, goes directly to the parents of the workers. Sometimes the farmer pays for the labor in advance, or offers a loan, charging the parents interest of 1.5% to 2% a month. There may be deductions from the pay envelope for food. Boarding for migrant laborers is usually free—often a spot on the farmer's veranda or in a shed with fertilizers or on a rooftop, next to the drying cotton.

The season starts with the sowing of seed, staggered over a three-month period that begins in April. Two months after a row is planted the bushes are in bloom and the real work begins. Pollen from male plants must be dusted by hand onto the flowers of female plants. The pollination work lasts for 70 to 100 days and is followed by cotton-picking staggered over several months. Children's hands are ideal for the delicate work with stamens and pistils. Their bodies are no better at withstanding the poisons. At least once a week, says Davuluri Venkateshwarlu, head of Glocal, farmers spray the fields with pesticides like Nuvacron, banned by the U.S. Environmental Protection Agency, and endosulfan, methomyl and Metasystox, considered by the EPA to be highly toxic. Venkateshwarlu ticks off the effects of overexposure: diarrhea, nausea, difficulty in breathing, convulsions, headaches and depression.

The farmers buy the starter seed from Monsanto at a cost that comes to the equivalent of $30 an acre. That acre will produce something like 900 pounds of cottonseed, to be sold back to Monsanto at $3.80 a pound, or $3,400 an acre. The cotton fiber is sold separately by a middleman.

In a magnanimous gesture that accomplished nothing, the Indian government cracked down on the seed companies by putting a ceiling on the cost of the starter seed (it used to be $64 an acre) but did nothing to change the price paid for the product seed, which was left to the seed companies. The product price has remained essentially flat in rupee terms over the past six years, despite 4.7% average annual inflation in India.

Big Numbers from Small Hands

Child labor is a global phenomenon. Still, some of the poorest regions of the world—and certain countries in particular—stand out for their reliance on work done by the underaged. The figures above the pie charts represent the total number of children age 5 to 14 in that country, except for Bolivia and India; those figures represent children age 7 to 14. The pie charts show the percentage of child laborers.

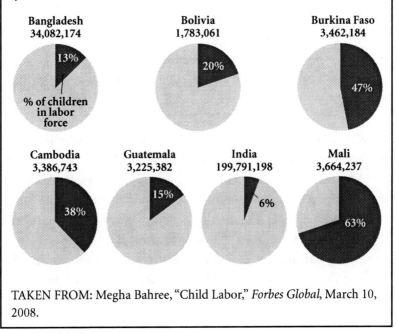

TAKEN FROM: Megha Bahree, "Child Labor," *Forbes Global,* March 10, 2008.

Farmers say their cost squeeze forces them to use child labor. "That allegation is not true," says Monsanto spokesperson Lee Quarles. "Indian cottonseed producers actually realize almost seven times the financial benefits growing cottonseed for local seed companies than if they were to sell that same yield at farm gate prices"—using their land, that is, primarily to produce cotton rather than seed.

In the neighboring states of Karnataka, Maharashtra and Gujarat, you find children producing genetically modified seeds for such vegetables as okra, tomatoes, chilies and eggplant, in the service of Syngenta, says Venkateshwarlu. The tomato and chili flowers are even smaller and more delicate than the cotton buds. The pesticides are more frequently applied, Venkateshwarlu says, and the pay is less, 5 to 10 cents an hour, even though the mandated minimum wage is 17 cents. Not so, Syngenta insists. "Our contracts require payment of minimum wage," says Anne Burt, a spokesperson, adding that Syngenta has a strict policy against child labor. The seeds are sold to U.S. farmers, the tomatoes and eggplant to U.S. consumers.

Farmers say their cost squeeze forces them to use child labor.

Monsanto, Syngenta and Bayer, all working under the glare of labor monitors like Glocal, are grappling with ways to prevent the abuse of children. They have, in fact, a symbiotic relationship with these outside groups, sometimes paying them to keep watch over the fields or scold parents into sending their children to school. Monsanto says if it finds a farmer employing children, it cans him. But in interviews farmers say that happens only after a third offense. "The problem," says Mohammad Raheemuddin of the MV Foundation in Hyderabad, "is that too few people have been assigned to monitor a vast area."

"One reason [monitoring groups] are so important in India is because the government has been an utter failure in implementing the law," says Zama Coursen-Neff, deputy director at Human Rights Watch in New York City. "But in any situation where there's funding available there is room for corruption and abuse." (See box)

At the very least, the watchdogs have learned to exploit the media. Sometimes they tip off journalists before persuading the police to raid a sweatshop. In October 2007 the New Delhi NGO Bachpan Bachao Andolan informed the *Observer*, the British daily, that 14 kids, some as young as 10, were spending

16 hours a day at a subcontractor embroidering blouses for GapKids. Gap, which has canned the subcontractor, placed its vendor on probation and cut its orders, recently met with suppliers to underscore its zero-tolerance policy and created a $200,000 grant to improve workshop conditions.

The labor organizations can't agree on how to ameliorate the situation. Some say that children of poor families have to work in order to make ends meet and that the government should offer them night classes to prepare them for better jobs. Others want to end child labor by finding jobs for parents, thereby eliminating the necessity for kids to work. "There is obviously a demand for labor," says labor economist Ashok Khandelwal, who works with unions. "But if a child is working that [usually] means the parents aren't."

Seven-year-old Santosh hadn't been in her new job a week yet in Dabbi, in the western desert state of Rajasthan, when a reporter visited. Chiseling quarry waste into blocks, she hurt her thumb and several fingers while figuring out how to hold a piece of sandstone in place with her foot in order to shape it to the desired size. India is the third-largest exporter of decorative stone—marble, granite, slate, sandstone—after Italy and China, with $1.2 billion in export revenue in fiscal 2006. Her work will likely end up in the garden and patio shops of American retail chains.

"We mandate an age of 16 or older," says Karen Cobb, speaking for Lowe's. "Our inspections cover quarries and have found that our vendors are in compliance with our standards."

In a nine-hour workday [Leela, aged 10] can . . . earn $1.26.

Laborers get paid by the cobble—a penny for a piece of 8 square inches, 7 cents for one of 66 square inches. Children are ideal because of their flexible hands and gentle pressure on the chisel and the hammer, says Rana Sengupta with the Mine Labor Protection Campaign (Trust) in Rajasthan. Hammer bruises are as common as cuts from flying pieces of the stone or slices from the chisel. So, too, says Sengupta, are silicosis, tuberculosis and bronchitis from inhaling dust particles.

Leela, 10, has been at this work for two years now. In a nine-hour workday she can turn out 50 pieces and earn $1.26. She takes two days off a month. At another Rajasthan quarry, 15-year-old Raju has spent his adolescence among the piles of sandstone waste. He dropped out of school four years ago to make cobbles. He's become something of a veteran. "I used to get hit by these broken pieces in my shins all the time," Raju says. "But with practice I finally got it right." Occasionally a piece of the chisel breaks and flies off like shrapnel. Raju points to a worker who has such a wound, just under his ribs. "It doesn't hurt," he assures.

Further north, in the state of Uttar Pradesh, hand-knotted carpets are made and sent to showrooms in the U.S. Such goods can be found, says Washington, D.C., NGO Rugmark, at Bloomingdale's, ABC Carpet & Home and Ikea. The chains insist they do not tolerate child labor. In Mirzapur most looms are inside people's homes or in communal sheds. Workers live and sleep in the same low-slung sheds, stepping down into 3-foot-deep trenches dug into the earthen floors to house the looms. Two or three people sit at a loom. The pits get damp, especially during the monsoons, and after the daylight fades, weavers must rely on a single naked lightbulb.

For the past year 14-year-old Rakil Momeen has been working at a loom in a shack in Mirzapur. A fourth-grade dropout, he left his parents in West Bengal and trekked halfway across the country. In his new life he works from 6 a.m. to 11 p.m. and earns $25 a month. After every knot the threads must be cut precisely with a sharp, curved blade. Rakil complains, not about nicks in fingers, but about homesickness. His face lights up as he remembers his childhood in the Malda district. "I used to hang out with my friends and my parents all the time," he says. "I really miss that." A cricket fan, he keeps his worn-out cricket bat next to him at the loom; occasionally he gets to play a game on Sundays.

India is full of painful incongruities. In the capital, on Asaf Ali Road, just across from the Delhi Stock Exchange and behind a wall of tiny storefronts, is a maze of alleyways 2 feet wide, with exposed rooms on both sides. In some places rickety metal ladders go three floors high to the rooftop. Crammed into rooms no bigger than a king-size bed, six to eight young boys, some as young as 5 years old, are hard at work. They're decorating photo frames, diaries, shoe heels and such with sequins and pieces of glass. You can find similar items at stores like Pier 1 and Target, says Athreya of Labor Rights Forum. The companies insist that their vendors not employ underage children.

In one such room, where the only piece of furniture is a low workbench, 10-year-old Akbar sits on the floor and mixes two powders into a doughy adhesive, his fingers blackened by the chemicals. Another boy spreads a thin layer of the mixture on a photo frame and a third, seated on his haunches, starts pasting tiny pieces of mirrors and sequins along the border. He sways back and forth, a habit most kids have developed to keep the blood flowing through their limbs as they sit for several hours. Decorating one 5-by-5-inch frame consumes six child-hours. The boys, who all live in the room and cook their own food here, typically work from 9 a.m. to 1 a.m. for $76 a month. Many have teeth stained from cigarettes they smoke and tobacco they chew to relieve the tedium.

Sometime within the next few months Gap intends to convene a global forum to consider "industrywide solutions" to child labor. Good luck. Since October Gap has cut in half its orders from a contractor in New Delhi it claims had subcontracted embroidery work out to an unofficial vendor without the company's knowledge. But in the wake of the bust, middlemen have found new ways to duck responsibility by removing labels that identify the origin of apparel. Says Bhuwan Ribhu, whose organization, Bachpan Bacho Andolan, helped bust the subcontractor, "Now it's even harder to trace who the shipment is for and to hold the companies accountable."

Myths About Child Labor Abound

Global March Against Child Labour

In the following viewpoint, Global March Against Child Labour has identified seven common myths about child labor. Foremost is that child labor is necessitated by poverty. Studies show that some poor countries have far less child labor than more affluent ones. Global March supports every child's right to an education, asserting that education, not child labor, is the key toward building stronger national economies. Putting children to work is a violation of their fundamental rights to live happy, healthy lives. There are no circumstances, Global March contends, in which child labor has proven to be more valuable than educating a child. Global March Against Child Labour is a movement to promote worldwide efforts to defend the rights of children.

As you read, consider the following questions:

1. According to Global March, what other factors cause child labor besides poverty?
2. Why is the notion that children gain skills, and thus benefit later in life, from working at an early age incorrect?
3. According to Global March, are children significantly cheaper to hire than adults?

*M*yth 1: *Children have to work because of poverty.*

Admittedly, most child laborers come from poor families. However, poverty is not the only reason children work, nor is it as central as many people think. Recent studies examining the role poverty plays in child labor have found that other factors, such as *parents' low regard for the education of children*, particularly girls, and *failing education systems* contribute equally to child labor. Too often poverty is used as an *excuse* for child labor. Yet, it is a myth that child labor will never be eliminated until poverty is eradicated. Conversely, poverty will never be eradicated until child laborers are redirected to schools. Child labor perpetuates poverty.

While economic development tends to reduce child labor in the long run, poverty does *not* necessarily induce child labor or hinder children from attending school. The picture varies. In many *poor* households, some children (particularly boys) are singled out to attend school. Additionally, there are states within *less* developed countries where child labor is not extensively practiced. For instance, Kerala State in India has virtually abolished child labor.

Too often poverty is used as an excuse *for child labor.*

At the country-level, a country may be *poor*, yet have relatively *low* levels of child labor compared to higher-income countries. For example, in 2001 only 18.5 percent of children ages 10–14 years were economically active in Yemen—a low-income country—whereas in 2000, 45.3 percent of children ages 6–14 years worked in Lebanon—an upper-middle-income country. The incidence of child labor can be relatively low even at fairly low levels of national income. For example, in 1999 an estimated 15 percent of children ages 5–14 worked in Sri Lanka—a low-middle-income country.

Thus, the relationship between economic development and child labor is *not* necessarily linear. While economic growth facilitates the reduction of child labor, the reduction of child labor contributes to development. Thus, the connection between child labor and economic development runs both ways.

Myth 2: Poor families need children to contribute economically to their survival.

When the topic of the elimination of child labor is raised, people often immediately object saying, "How will poor families survive without the additional income of the children?" Perhaps no concern about the desire to eliminate child labor is more rampant than the perception that *households, particularly those in poverty, cannot afford to lose the contribution made by their children.* Household poverty is widely regarded to be *the* chief cause of child labor. However, this is not necessarily true. As myth #1 indicates, other factors may be at work as well. Initially, some families have difficulty coping without the wages of their children. However, removing children from work may not present as much of a problem as initially perceived. Redirecting child laborers to school is better for families in the long run than letting them continue to work.

Regrettably, there is little systematic evidence regarding the economic value of child labor. Income from children typically accounts for some 10–40 percent of household income, which might be critical when household income is so low that it is spent mostly on food. In its *2003 Economic Study of the Costs and Benefits of Eliminating Child Labor*, ILO-IPEC [International Labour Organization—International Programme on the Elimination of Child Labour] assumes that a child worker's contribution to household income is 20 percent of an adult's contribution. While child labor may increase household-income and contribute to its survival in the short run, it tends to have the opposite effect for future generations.

Myth 3: Children are better suited for some work than adults; they provide irreplaceable skills (for example, nimble fingers and dexterity).

Historically, it has been believed that children are better suited for some kinds of work than adults. This is commonly used as an excuse for using child labor in the carpet weaving industry, e.g., children's "nimble fingers" make it possible for them to tie smaller and tighter knots. Yet, evidence negates the idea that children make better workers than adults because they are endowed with special attributes that are superior to adults for particular work. Research carried out by the International Labor Organization has proved that this claim is often indefensible. The "nimble fingers" argument is entirely wrong in several hazardous industries, including carpet-making, glass manufacturing, mining, and gem polishing. Even in hand-knotting of carpets, which calls for considerable dexterity, an empirical study of over 2,000 weavers found that children were no more likely than adults to make the finest knots. Some of the best carpets, with the greatest density of small knots, are woven by adults. If a child's "nimble fingers" are not essential in such demanding work, it is difficult to imagine in which trades this claim might be valid.

Redirecting child laborers to school is better for families in the long run than letting them continue to work.

Myth 4: Child labor is needed for development or economic growth.

There is no evidence to support the theory that children must work for a *thriving* industry until economic growth and technological advancements replace them. Historically, the *elimination* of child labor and its replacement with universal education has contributed to the economic growth of countries. Child labor reflects underinvestment in education and the future of a nation. *Education* is at the heart of development. Historically, *the universal completion of free education of good quality* has been identified as the key to economic growth. As long as 246 million children aged 5–17 are working how can they attend school? Child laborers are automatically denied their right to education. Clearly, Education for All will never be achieved if the needs of child laborers are unmet. Child labor hinders the full development of human capital. A less skilled workforce results in low productivity and income for countries.

Many studies have recognized the historical link between the reduction of child labor, the increase in school attendance, and the economic growth of industrialized countries. Both the enactment of mandatory education laws and the provision of schools have naturally helped to reduce child labor and are *pre*conditions for rapid economic growth. Educational attainment has played an important role in the rapid economic growth of many countries in East Asia, such as Korea.

Myth 5: Child labor is a valuable part of children's early childhood education.

Millions of child laborers miss a critical time in their physical and mental development to work day and night. Primary and secondary education imparts not only the knowledge and skills children need to obtain adequate employment as adults, but also provides children with an opportunity to relate to people in social settings. Moreover, education empowers children by enabling them to gain knowledge of their basic rights and realize their potential.

Findings disprove the claim that children benefit later in life from working at a young age. Child laborers often end up draining national economies. With no to little education, they grow up to be less healthy and less productive than adults who did not work until they reached adulthood. Findings using data from Brazil demonstrate that entry into the workforce before age 13 years *reduces* adult lifetime earnings by 13–17 percent, and increases the probability of persons falling

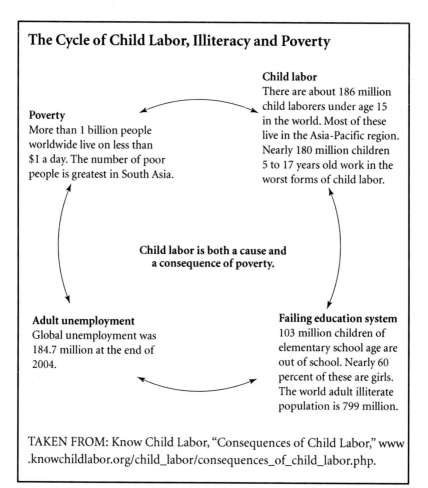

The Cycle of Child Labor, Illiteracy and Poverty

Child labor
There are about 186 million child laborers under age 15 in the world. Most of these live in the Asia-Pacific region. Nearly 180 million children 5 to 17 years old work in the worst forms of child labor.

Poverty
More than 1 billion people worldwide live on less than $1 a day. The number of poor people is greatest in South Asia.

Child labor is both a cause and a consequence of poverty.

Adult unemployment
Global unemployment was 184.7 million at the end of 2004.

Failing education system
103 million children of elementary school age are out of school. Nearly 60 percent of these are girls. The world adult illiterate population is 799 million.

TAKEN FROM: Know Child Labor, "Consequences of Child Labor," www .knowchildlabor.org/child_labor/consequences_of_child_labor.php.

to the bottom percent of the income distribution later in life by 7–8 percent. Results suggest that policies that *delay* the age of entry into work may have significant positive impacts on adult incidence of poverty.

Child laborers often end up draining national economies.

Myth 6: Children have the "right" to decent work.

Some groups advocate protecting the right of children to work and to bargain for better working conditions. However, the very concept of children working violates standards set by international conventions related to children. A child's rights are non-negotiable. All children are equally entitled to their rights without discrimination, regardless of their economic, social or biological background. Their need to work because of economic necessity, or other reasons, does not create a new children's "right" to work replacing their rights to education, play, and protection from economic exploitation. Forcing children to work for their own survival is society's *refutation* of their fundamental rights.

Govind, a former child laborer from Nepal and a current activist with the South Asian Coalition Against Child Servitude (SACCS) in India says, "We want a world where the same system works for *all* children. I have heard that some people are talking about the right of children to work. I do not understand how those people are thinking against the feelings of children. Are they ready to send their own children to work? Who gave these people the right to make children their way of business?"

"I have heard that some people are talking about the right of children to work. I do not understand how those people are thinking against the feelings of children."

Myth 7: Children are "cheaper"; they cost less to hire.

The "economic" argument that it costs much less to employ children than adults collapses under close scrutiny. Children are usually paid less than adults. Yet, the International Labor Organization has found that the *labor-cost savings* from the use of child labor is very *small*: less than 5 percent compared to the final foreign retail price of bangles; and less than 5–10 percent compared to the final foreign retail price of carpets. Foreign retailers typically mark up carpets approximately 200 percent. Carpets can easily cost four times as much to the consumer as the Indian export price.

Child Domestic Workers Are Often Mistreated

Human Rights Watch

According to the non-governmental organization Human Rights Watch, children who work as domestics in private homes are a neglected and often abused segment of child laborers. Child domestic workers are found in countries as diverse as Guatemala, Malaysia, and Togo. Because these child workers labor in relative isolation in the homes of their employers, they are subject to a wide range of abuses, including underpayment, long hours, and even sexual abuse, with little or no public scrutiny. Human Rights Watch asserts that child domestics must be accorded the same rights as any other workers, that all children must have access to an education, and that children must not be subjected to harmful or dangerous working conditions. Human Rights Watch conducts research and advocates for human rights around the world, and has been active in issues such as child labor, torture, genocide, and capital punishment.

As you read, consider the following questions:

1. In which countries has Human Rights Watch conducted investigations of child domestic labor?

2. According to Human Rights Watch, how many Indonesian women work in Malaysia as household domestics?

"Child Domestics: The World's Invisible Workers: A Human Rights Watch Backgrounder," Human Rights Watch, June 10, 2004. http://hrw.org. Reproduced by permission.

3. Under international law, why is child labor not prohibited?

Child domestic workers are nearly invisible among child laborers. They work alone in individual households, hidden from public scrutiny, their lives controlled by their employers. Child domestics, nearly all girls, work long hours for little or no pay. Many have no opportunity to go to school, or are forced to drop out because of the demands of their job. They are subject to verbal and physical abuse, and particularly vulnerable to sexual abuse. They may be fired for small infractions, losing not only their jobs, but their place of residence as well.

The International Labor Organization (ILO) estimates that more girls work as domestics than in any other form of child labor. Yet they have received little attention, and even less protection. Government laws often exclude domestic workers from basic labor rights, labor ministries rarely monitor or investigate conditions of work in private households, and few programs addressing child labor include child domestics.

In independent investigations in West Africa (2002), Guatemala (2000), El Salvador (2003), and Malaysia/Indonesia (2004), Human Rights Watch found that child domestics are exploited and abused on a routine basis. Despite the striking differences between these countries, the daily realities of the children are remarkably similar.

Child Domestics in Central America

The señor wanted to take advantage of me, he followed me around . . . he grabbed my breasts twice from behind while I was washing clothes in the pila. I yelled, and the boy came out, and the señor left. I didn't tell the señora, because I was afraid. I just quit.

—Mariá A., Guatemala,
describing an incident when she was fourteen or fifteen

In Guatemala and El Salvador tens of thousands of girls work as domestics, some as young as eight years old. Human Rights Watch found that domestic workers often labor over fifteen hours a day, or ninety hours a week, for wages much lower than those of other workers. Like domestics in most other countries, they are routinely subject to verbal and emotional abuse from their employers, and are particularly vulnerable to sexual harassment and sexual violence from men living in or associated with the household.

According to one local advocate in Guatemala, employers control nearly every aspect of a domestic worker's life, including "the salary she earns, the work she does, her working hours, the days she can go out, where she can go and even what language she should speak in the home and how she should dress."

In Guatemala and El Salvador tens of thousands of girls work as domestics, some as young as eight years old.

Domestic work frequently interferes with schooling. Many domestics have no opportunity to attend school. Others drop out, most commonly because their work hours conflict with the school day or because of school fees and other education-related expenses. Some are able to attend night classes, but traveling to and from school at night involves increased risks to their safety.

Seventeen-year-old Flor N. works thirteen hours each day as a domestic worker in San Salvador, beginning at 4:30 a.m. "It's heavy work: washing, ironing, taking care of the child," she told Human Rights Watch. When she finishes her workday, she heads to her fifth grade evening class. "Sometimes I come to school super tired. . . . I get up at 2 a.m. to go to work." When she rises at 2 a.m. to return to work, she must walk one kilometer along a dangerous road to catch a minibus. The only domestic worker for a household of four adults and a three-year-old, she is also responsible for preparing their lunch, dinner, and snacks, and she watches the child. "Sometimes I eat, but sometimes I am too busy," she told us. "There is no rest for me. I can sit, but I have to be doing something." She has only one day off each month and receives wages of about U.S.$26/month for her labor.

Many domestics have no opportunity to attend school.

In Guatemala, most domestic workers migrate from rural villages to work in urban households. Many are Mayan, and are routinely subject to ethnic discrimination. A Keqchikel [a cultural sub-group of the Mayans] girl told Human Rights Watch that when she was fourteen, she worked seventeen hours a day, with only ten minutes to eat lunch and dinner. Her employers gave her "a different class of food" than they ate themselves, and would not let her eat near them. "They treated me poorly because I wear traje (traditional dress)," she said.

One third of the domestic workers Human Rights Watch interviewed in Guatemala reported having suffered some kind of unwanted sexual approaches by men living in or associated with the household. Few domestic workers feel they can tell the woman of the house about such abuse; most simply quit and look for another job.

Both the Guatemalan and Salvadoran labor codes effectively exclude domestics from basic labor rights. Unlike most other workers, they are denied the nationally recognized eight-hour workday. Domestics commonly receive wages that are lower than the minimum wages in other sectors of employment.

Salvadoran government officials often deny that children, particularly those under the minimum employment age of fourteen, work in domestic service in large numbers. An ILO study on work in domestic service concluded that it was among the worst forms of child labor, but the Salvadoran government has not included domestic labor in its ILO Time-Bound Program, an initiative to eliminate the worst forms of child labor within a period of five to ten years.

Child Domestics in Indonesia and Malaysia

I took care of two children. . . . I cleaned all parts of the house, washed the floor, washed clothes, ironed, cleaned the walls, and washed the car. I cleaned two houses, because I also cleaned the grandmother's house. I worked from 4 a.m. to 7 p.m. I had no rest during the day. I worked every day and was not allowed to go out, not even to walk on the street. The lady employer yelled at me every day. She slapped me one or two times a week. My employer kept my passport. I was scared to run away without my passport. I wanted to run away, but I was afraid the Malaysian government and security would catch me. I had to buy my own ticket home. [When I returned to Indonesia,] I called the labor recruitment company in Jakarta to complain about my salary, but they didn't want to take my call.

—Srihati H., seventeen years old,
former Indonesian migrant domestic worker in Malaysia

Approximately 200,000 Indonesian girls and women work in Malaysia as household domestics. Human Rights Watch interviews in 2004 with Indonesian migrant workers, Indonesian government officials, and labor agents suggest that many girls migrate for work abroad with altered ages on their travel documents, masking the number of girls in official statistics. Suwari S. told Human Rights Watch, "There were a lot of young girls [in the labor recruitment training center], the youngest was fifteen. They changed my age to twenty-six; I was sixteen at the time."

Child domestic workers encounter abuses at every stage of the migration process, including recruitment, training, employment, and return. Indonesian girls seeking employment abroad encounter unscrupulous labor agents, discriminatory hiring processes, and months-long confinement in overcrowded training centers. In order to pay recruitment and processing fees, they either take large loans requiring repayment at extremely high interest rates or the first four or five months of their salary is deducted. Labor recruiters often fail to provide complete information about job responsibilities, work conditions, or where the girls can turn for help if they face abuse. Girls expecting to spend one month in predeparture training facilities are often trapped in heavily guarded centers for three to six months without any income, or may be trafficked into forced labor, including forced domestic work or forced sex work.

Child domestic workers encounter abuses at every stage of the migration process, including recruitment, training, employment, and return.

Once employed as domestic workers in Malaysia, Indonesian girls and women typically work sixteen-hour days, seven days a week, with no overtime pay and with no scheduled rest. Domestic workers in Malaysia are not allowed outside of the house and many reported they were unable to write letters home, make phone calls, or practice their religion. Many employers withhold payment of wages until the standard two-year contract is completed, making it difficult for girls to escape from abusive situations. At the end of the contract, many do not receive their full wages, and if they do, receive U.S.$90-100 per month, amounting to less than $0.25 per hour. Employers and labor agents routinely confiscate the passports of domestic workers, making it difficult for them to escape. The rigid enforcement of Malaysia's draconian immigration laws mean that workers caught without documents are often indefinitely detained and deported without being able to present their complaints about abusive employers.

Abuses against child domestics are compounded by the lack of legal protection for domestic workers in Malaysia's employment laws, and the limited possibilities for redress. Malaysia's employment laws specifically exclude basic labor protections for domestic workers, including those governing hours of work, rest days, and compensation for accidents. There are no mechanisms for monitoring workplace conditions, and the resolution of most abuse cases is left to private, profit-motivated labor agencies often guilty of committing abuses themselves. Bilateral labor agreements between Indonesia and Malaysia fail to provide adequate protections for domestic workers, and do not include protections for child workers. Malaysia and Indonesia have both ratified ILO Convention 182 on the Prohibition of the Worst Forms of Child Labor, but enforcement remains weak.

Child Domestics in West and Central Africa

In the beginning, she [my boss] was nice to me, but then she changed. Any time I did something wrong, she would shout at me and insult me. Sometimes she would tell her friends what I had done, and they would come over and beat me. . . . She would curse me and say I had no future.

—*Assoupi H., sixteen,*
a child domestic worker in [the West African country] Togo

In west and central Africa, girls as young as seven provide a cheap workforce to families needing assistance with housework or small commercial trades. They work long days performing a variety of tasks, such as selling bread, fruit or milk in the market, grilling skewers of meat on the roadside, or working in a small boutique. Some describe selling bread in the market from 6 a.m. until 7 p.m, then returning home to bake bread for the next day. Others are forced to spend all day pounding *fufu*, a doughy paste made of mashed yams or cassava. When not working in markets, girls perform domestic

Child Domestic Servants

▓ Countries that have high rates
of child domestic servants

TAKEN FROM: Fisek Institute, http://www.fisek.org.

chores such as preparing meals, washing dishes, or caring for young children. One sixteen-year old girl was trafficked to Togo when she was only three. "I had to fetch water for the house, sweep, wash the dishes, and wash clothes," she said. "I would bathe the children, cook for them, and wash their clothes. When they were young, they cried a lot."

Child domestics work under constant threat of punishment and physical abuse. "If I lost any yam in the pounding, the woman beat me—slapped me with her hand," a Togolese girl reported. Another said, "If we didn't sell all the bread in one day, she [the boss] would beat us with a stick." In interviews with Human Rights Watch, girls described being struck with blunt objects and electric wire, and threatened with punishment and sometimes death. Many escaped following an incident of unendurable abuse, after which they lived abandoned in the street. Girls also faced the risk of sexual abuse by older men or boys living in the same house or when living in the street.

Child domestic work is linked to the broader phenomenon of child trafficking, which occurs along numerous routes in west and central Africa. The United Nations estimates that 200,000 children are recruited for labor exploitation each year in the region that includes Benin, Burkina Faso, Cameroon, Cote D'Ivoire, Gabon, Ghana, Mali, Nigeria, and Togo. Child traffickers capitalize on a combination of entrenched poverty and weak child protection laws, as well as a high demand for cheap labor in host countries. Children orphaned by HIV/ AIDS or other causes may be disproportionately vulnerable due to the stigma they face, as well as the economic pressures caused by the loss of a breadwinner. Child trafficking is also linked to the denial of education, especially for girls, who may be the first to be withdrawn from school to earn a living. A number of children report that the prohibitive cost of school supplies or uniforms forces them to withdraw from school, after which they are recruited by child traffickers.

Child domestics work under constant threat of punishment and physical abuse.

Some countries in the region have enacted anti-trafficking legislation in compliance with the U.N. Protocol to Prevent, Suppress and Punish the Trafficking of Persons (2000), but such laws remain poorly enforced. Gabonese authorities reportedly conduct periodic roundups of child laborers and arrange for their repatriation to their country of origin. Employers and traffickers are rarely prosecuted, however. While some bilateral and multilateral repatriation agreements exist, efforts to negotiate a regional anti-trafficking convention stalled in 2002. Governments also fail to provide adequate protection to trafficked children. While some short-term shelters exist, follow-up and rehabilitation are rarely conducted, and a lack of child protection measures often allows children to be re-trafficked multiple times.

Child Labor Under International Law

Under international law, child labor in itself is not prohibited, in recognition of the potential benefits of some forms of work and of the realities that require many children to enter the workforce to support their own or their families' basic needs. Instead, international treaties address the circumstances under which children may work and require states to set minimum ages for employment. In addition, children who work do not give up the basic human rights that all children are guaranteed; in particular, they continue to enjoy the right to education.

The International Prohibition on Harmful or Hazardous Child Labor: The Convention on the Rights of the Child, ratified by all countries except Somalia and the United States, guarantees children the right "to be protected from performing any work that is likely to be hazardous or to interfere with the child's education, or to be harmful to the child's health or physical, mental, spiritual, moral or social development."

The Worst Forms of Child Labour Convention, adopted by the International Labour Organization (ILO) in 1999, and ratified by 150 countries worldwide, develops the prohibition on harmful or hazardous work more fully. Under the Worst Forms of Child Labour Convention, some forms of child labor are flatly prohibited, such as slavery or practices similar to slavery. Other types of work are prohibited if they constitute "work which, by its nature or the circumstances in which it is carried out, is likely to harm the health, safety or morals of children."

ILO recommendations for what constitutes hazardous labor under the Worst Forms of Child Labour Convention includes work that "exposes children to physical, psychological or sexual abuse" or involves "particularly difficult conditions such as work for long hours or during the night or work where the child is unreasonably confined to the premises of the employer." Under these criteria, most child domestic work would constitute hazardous labor and should be prohibited.

The Right to Education: The Convention on the Rights of the Child guarantees children's right to education, stating that primary education must be "compulsory and available free to all." Secondary education, including vocational education, must be "available and accessible to every child," with the progressive introduction of free secondary education. With regard to the interplay between child labor and education, the Convention on the Rights of the Child explicitly guarantees children the right "to be protected from performing any work that is likely . . . to interfere with the child's education. . . ."

The Convention for the Elimination of All Forms of Discrimination Against Women (CEDAW) provides for the elimination of discrimination against girls in education, including access to schooling, reduction of female student drop-out rates, and programs for girls who have left school prematurely.

Protecting the Rights of Child Domestics

The large numbers of girls working as domestic laborers, and the extreme exploitation and abuse that they endure requires that the international community prioritize protection for child domestics as part of strategies to end child labor. Key steps that governments can take to protect the rights of child domestics include the following:

- Establishing an unequivocal minimum age for employment and explicitly prohibiting the employment of all children under the age of eighteen in harmful or hazardous labor.

- Amending national laws as necessary to ensure that domestic workers receive the same rights as other workers, including a minimum wage, time off, and limits on hours of work.

- Launching public information campaigns on the rights of domestic workers and responsibilities of employers, with special emphasis on the situation of child domestic workers and the potential hazards they face.

- Ensuring that all children enjoy the right to a free basic education by eliminating formal school fees and other obstacles to education, and by identifying and implementing strategies to reduce other costs to attending school, such as transportation, school supplies, and uniforms.

- Creating a confidential toll-free hotline to receive reports of workers' rights violations, including abuses against child domestics.

- Creating effective mechanisms for inspection, enforcement, and monitoring of child labor, and promptly investigating any complaints of abuses against child domestics.

- Taking all appropriate law enforcement measures against perpetrators of physical and/or sexual violence against child domestics.

- Ensuring care and support to children who escape domestic labor and have suffered physical or sexual violence, including treatment of sexually transmitted diseases.

In South Asia, Carpets Are Made Using Child Labor

The Anti-Slavery Society

Despite assertions that child labor in the carpet industry is a thing of the past, in the following viewpoint the Anti-Slavery Society maintains that hundreds of thousands of children continue to labor in near-slavery conditions in the rug-producing nations of India, Pakistan, and Nepal. These children work in abysmal conditions and earn pitiful wages. The Anti-Slavery Society acknowledges that adults make the finest carpets, but children make low- to middle-grade rugs. A growing movement in these countries is working to end child labor, the authors assert, and the governments must contribute to that effort by enforcing child labor laws. The Anti-Slavery Society, which originated in 1983, is a non-governmental agency that aims to relieve the suffering, to free or rescue, and to effect the social reintegration of slaves, child slaves, bonded laborers, and other such victims.

As you read, consider the following questions:

1. According to the Anti-Slavery Society, why doesn't the average consumer realize that children are still involved in the carpet making industry?
2. According to the article, is the claim that fine carpets require tiny hands to make them legitimate?
3. Who generally controls the carpet industry?

"Child Labor in the Carpet Industry," Anti-Slavery Society, Anti-slaverysociety.addr.com, April 3, 2007. Reproduced by permission.

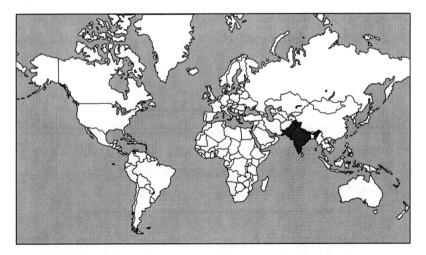

Carpet manufacturers and the carpet export industry in Pakistan, as well as carpet importers and retailers in the USA and other Western countries, have announced that child labor no longer exists in the carpet-weaving industry. They have attacked UNICEF [United Nations Children's Fund], the [Anti-Slavery] Society and other charities as "do-gooders", the phrase used by the Chief Executive Officer of the largest carpet importer in the United Kingdom.

The ordinary American consumer, with family commitments and a mortgage, does not have the time and money to travel to Pakistan to verify these claims.

Who do you believe?

UNICEF and the other charities like this Society have no financial interest in making such claims. The carpet industry does.

Children Are Still Extensively Used

Since these claims have been made by the industry, the Society has funded a Mission to Pakistan which shows the extensive use of children in the industry. Many of them . . . are very young. . . .

A recent undercover investigation in Pakistan by the Society ... revealed that young children still work in horrific conditions making carpets which we buy and put in our homes. . . .

In India the South Asian Coalition on Child Servitude estimates that between 200,000 and 300,000 children are involved [in the carpet industry], most of them in the carpet belt of Uttar Pradesh in central India.

The handmade woolen carpet industry is extremely labor intensive and one of the largest export earners for India, Pakistan, Nepal and Morocco. During the past 20 years, it has been one of the fastest growing industries and most of this growth has been achieved through the use of child labor.

The total number of children involved in the industry in South Asia is very difficult to assess, but in India the South Asian Coalition on Child Servitude estimates that between 200,000 and 300,000 children are involved, most of them in the carpet belt of Uttar Pradesh in central India.

Similar numbers may be working in Pakistan and up to 150,000 in Nepal.

For years the industry claimed in its propaganda that the nimble fingers of children are essential to form the intricate designs used in the carpets.

This claim has long been discredited and the most expensive carpets are generally made by adults, with children producing the low and middle grade carpets.

Why Carpets Makers Use Children

There are two main advantages of child labor to the carpet makers:

- their very low wages and their docile acceptance of terrible working conditions;

- their good eyesight, which allows them to perform intricate work in very poor light.

Harm to Children

As a result, many of the children, who may begin working as young as 6 or 7 years old, are severely ill by the time they are adults.

Their eyesight is damaged and lung diseases are common as a result of the dust and fluff from the wool used in the carpets.

To make matters worse, many of the children employed in the industry have been separated from their families.

Many of the children, who may begin working as young as 6 or 7 years old, are severely ill by the time they are adults.

The carpet industry is very complex, but is generally controlled by the export companies. These exporters arrange, either directly or through contractors, for a carpet to be produced on a particular loom. The looms are normally owned by small entrepreneurs and range from single looms in private houses to small factories with 30 or more looms. The exporter supplies the wool and design and after a price and quality is agreed, the loom owner is responsible for producing the carpet to specification. Agents for the loom masters and owners find their workforce from a variety of sources.

The children may be their own children and other children from within the village. These remain in their own family.

The child labor may also be obtained from other areas (normally poorer regions) by purchasing or coercing children

The Rugmark Foundation

The [Anti-Slavery] Society is promoting "Rugmark" carpets—hand-woven carpets, which carry a guarantee against the use of child labor—in preference to carpets made by children (some as young as four years of age).

In August 1994, the Rugmark Foundation was registered in India by a consortium comprising ... business associations and human rights organizations. ... Exporters wishing to use the Rugmark have to register their looms with the Foundation and they will be checked by inspectors.

The "Rugmark" label on hand-knotted carpets from India indicates that they have not been produced by child labor. The conditions for use of the Rugmark are that the exporters undertake:

- [to] not use child labor in any area of production; and

- to pay all workers at least the minimum wage as set by Indian law.

It also requires regular school attendance by children working at home on family looms. The exporter will then be given the right to put a label on their carpets, which will carry a code enabling purchasers to check each carpet with the Foundation.

Anti-Slavery Society, "Fighting Slavery Today: Rugmark," 2008. www.anti-slaverysociety.addr.com.

from Bihar in north-east India to Uttar Pradesh; or from small villages in Nepal to Kathmandu; or from outlying villages to small towns in Pakistan; and even children trafficked from other countries, such as children imported from west

Nepal to Uttar Pradesh. Removed from their families, these are, without doubt, the worst sufferers.

Long Hours and Little Pay

All the children work long hours for very little pay. Indeed, in many cases, particularly when they live at the looms, their wages are reduced to pay for food and lodging, or they may receive no pay whatsoever, for example, where the loom owner applies their wages to cover the advances given to their parents and the agents who brought them in the first place. This is a form of debt bondage (which is defined as a slavery-like institution by Article 1(a) of Article 7(a) of the Supplementary Convention on the Abolition of Slavery, the Slave Trade and Institutions and Practices Similar to Slavery 1956) and is quite common in the industry throughout South Asia.

A great many of them are children who have been kidnapped by slavers from their parents and sold to the loom master.

They are locked behind bars and beaten. They are poorly fed and receive no wages.

In the past ten years, there has been a gathering movement in India, Pakistan and Nepal to end the exploitation of so many children in the industry. This activity has been supported by the Anti-Slavery Society. As a result, the UN [United Nations] Working Group on Contemporary Forms of Slavery and the International Labor Organization have called on the Union Government (i.e., the federal government) in India and the federal government in Pakistan to enforce their own laws and to stop the use of child labor.

Fine Carpets Are Not Made Using Child Labor

Lissa Wyman

In the following viewpoint, carpet expert Lissa Wyman relates a dispute with a volunteer guide at London's Victoria and Albert Museum. The guide had told the tour group that a magnificent carpet, a work of art, was fashioned by the hands of child laborers in the sixteenth century. According to Wyman, this could not be so. Young children do not possess the physical dexterity or mental acuity to weave such works of art, and a later visit by Wyman to several Pakistani rug facilities confirmed her suspicion that child labor is not used in the making of fine carpets. Lissa Wyman is rug editor for the magazine Furniture Today.

As you read, consider the following questions:

1. Why, according to Wyman, can't young children weave a fine rug?
2. Why did the docent claim that only child laborers could make the Ardabil Carpet?
3. Why did Wyman's husband "drag" her off before the argument could continue?

On my summer vacation, I got into a big argument with a docent [volunteer guide] at the Victoria & Albert Museum [V & A] in London—two middle-aged ladies having a hissy fit over the Ardabil Carpet.

Lissa Wyman, "The Myth of Tiny Fingers and Persian Rug Weaving," *Furniture Today*, vol. 31, no. 3, September 18, 2006, p. 34. Copyright © 2006 Reed Business Information, a division of Reed Elsevier Inc. All rights reserved. Reproduced by permission.

The Ardabil Carpet [a famous Persian carpet] has been re-mounted at the V&A. The lights where it's hung are dimmed for much of the time, brightening only every 20 minutes or so to illuminate this beautiful work of art. The guide gave a brief history then, eyeing a little girl in our group, she asked, "And do you know that this carpet was made by 10-year-old children!!?? Could you make a carpet like this?"

The little girl looked nervous.

I was seething.

A Myth Perpetuated

Why is this myth of child labor perpetuated? No 10-year-old child has the physical dexterity to knot a Persian-weave carpet. And unless 16th century kids were a heck of a lot smarter than those today, they didn't have the capacity for formal mathematical reasoning necessary to follow a carpet weaving pattern.

I approached the docent and thanked her for the lecture, told her who I was and asked her where she got her information about the 10-year-olds. Her response was the usual, simplistic one: "Only a person with tiny little fingers could make those little knots."

I explained the laws of physical and cognitive development and how they affect manual and intellectual dexterity, but she wasn't having any of it. "Maybe they had adult supervision, but it HAD to be children doing it," she said.

What is it about little fingers and rug weaving?

I think brain surgery is pretty intricate work, requiring tiny little stitches, but I'm not letting any 10-year-old kid near my head.

The V&A also exhibits fine examples of 16th century Gobelin [a French family of dyers] tapestries, with very tiny

How the Ardabil Carpet Was Made

The basic structure of the carpet is hidden by the pile. Like most textiles, it consists of warps and wefts. The warps are the threads running the length of the carpet. The wefts are the threads that run across its breadth. Both warps and wefts are made from silk, which is a very strong fibre when new. . . .

The pile is made from wool, which holds dye much better than silk. The pile is very dense—there are about 5300 knots per ten centimetres square (340 knots per square inch). This density allowed the designer to incorporate a great deal of detail, but making such a large carpet with so many knots would have taken a team of skilled weavers several years.

Up to ten weavers may have worked on the carpet at any one time. Most carpet weaving was done at home by women, but for a court commission such as this, the weavers may have been men.

"The Ardabil Carpet,"
Victoria and Albert Museum, www.vam.ac.uk.

stitches, and made at about the same time as the Ardabil Carpet. But no one talks about them being woven by Flemish children with tiny fingers.

I think brain surgery is pretty intricate work, requiring tiny little stitches, but I'm not letting any 10-year-old kid near my head.

My husband dragged me off before I got to that subject with the docent. "You can't change anyone's mind about a belief that goes so deep," he said.

He's probably right.

Grown Men Only

A couple weeks later, I went to Pakistan for a hand-knotted carpet exhibition. When I told my hosts about the cat fight at the V&A, they were appalled. I went to several hand-knotted carpet-making facilities in Lahore [the capital of the Pakistani province of Punjab]. The weavers were all grown men. Their hands and fingers weren't tiny. The only children I saw were in school uniforms. A 12-year-old boy at a carpet factory, the son of the plant foreman, looked like he was running some errands for his dad.

Maybe I can't change anyone's deeply held beliefs. But I can try.

West African Cocoa Farmers Use Child Slave Labor

Victoria Lambert

In the following viewpoint, Victoria Lambert writes that with help from fair trade foundations, cocoa farmers in Latin America are being taught how to maximize profits and survive downturns. This is not the case in West Africa, where many uneducated farmers rely on unpaid child labor—that is, child slaves—to work in the cocoa fields. Educating these farmers, Lambert asserts, would improve their lot as well as the lives of child laborers. While some corporations claim that they cannot influence the child labor situation on West African farms, other corporations are taking measures to ensure a more ethical method of chocolate production. Victoria Lambert is a British journalist who writes for the Daily Telegraph.

As you read, consider the following questions:

1. What percentage of the world's cocoa beans are produced in West Africa?
2. What topics are covered when cocoa farmers attend schools?
3. Why do chocolate manufacturers claim they cannot solve the child labor issue?

Victoria Lambert, "Choc Horror: With the Annual Chocolate-Mania of Easter Looming, the Spectre of Child Labour Still Hovers over the International Cocoa Industry," *Geographical*, vol. 80, no. 4, April 2008, pp. 86–87. Copyright © 2008 Circle Publishing Ltd. Reproduced by permission.

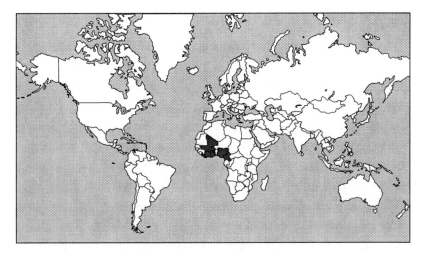

On his cocoa farm just outside Santo Domingo, the capital of the Dominican Republic, Christobel is a happy man. Ten years ago, he lost his entire crop to Hurricane George, which devastated much of the island in September 1998, leaving more than 100,000 people homeless. His own farm was ruined; his livelihood could have been destroyed for good.

Since then, as generations of farmers have done before him, Christobel, who is in his 50s, has replanted his crops over and over. And although he can't predict or prevent another hurricane, he's now more at ease with the future. These days, he's part of a Fairtrade Foundation scheme that has helped rebuild villages and homes, dug new wells and brought sanitation, and has not only improved the way cocoa beans—which grow in pods the size of rugby balls on trees—are farmed, but also stabilized the price. Moreover, the farmers are encouraged to grow fruit trees such as banana or mango over their beans, providing natural shade and creating a second cash crop. In this part of the world, the cocoa trade—worth US$5.1 billion worldwide—is being supported, nurtured and sustained. Sadly, this isn't the universal picture.

Cocoa Slaves

The greatest concern for chocolate lovers should be the continuing use of child labour on cocoa plantations in West Africa, where two million farms produce 70 per cent of the world's beans. According to the charity Save the Children Canada, more than 312,000 children are still working 'in the worst form of child labour in the fields.' Some are making a meager but essential contribution to their families—the price of cocoa has fallen to a quarter of its value ten years ago, which, combined with political instability, has led to acute poverty—but all are working in harsh conditions, and many, some as young as nine, are actively sold into slavery from countries such as Burkina Faso, Togo and Mali.

Figures compiled by the International Institute for Tropical Agriculture show that 64 per cent of plantation workers are less than 14 years old. Twelve thousand had no connection to the family on whose cocoa farm they toiled, but only 5,100 of them were paid for their work. Most worryingly, almost 6,000 were described as 'unpaid workers with no family ties'—to put it simply, slaves.

In 2000, when the television documentary *Slavery: A Global Investigation* revealed the extent of these abuses, particularly in Ghana and the Ivory Coast, there was widespread condemnation, with many governments promising to check the supply chain of any cocoa imported into their countries. Since then, there has been international pressure led by US Senator Tom Harkin to improve the situation, with countries encouraged to launch certification processes and survey the farms to determine what needs to be tackled. The original aim was that by 2005, the situation would have been cleaned up enough for chocolate manufacturers to label their products 'slave-free'.

But three years later, that seems like an empty promise. Rumours abound that slavery still exists not only in Africa but also in Brazil and Indonesia. Yet the cocoa industry seems satisfied that enough is being done, with Isabelle Adam, secretary general of the European Cocoa Association, saying: '[Ivory Coast] has made a serious, sustained commitment to tackling labour issues on cocoa farms.'

The original aim was that by 2005, the [child labour] situation would have been cleaned up enough for choco-late manufacturers to label their products 'slave-free'.

Save the Children Canada isn't so happy. It points out that it has waited five years for governments and the global choco-late industry to change child labour practices in the growing and harvesting of cocoa. It also wants proper tracking of the supply chain to be initiated.

'We must start with understanding where the cocoa in our chocolate comes from, and get choosy about whether or not we agree with the methods used to produce it,' says David Morley, president and CEO of Save the Children Canada. 'We're calling for greater investment in the communities where cocoa farms exist. We want governments, chocolate manufac-turers and individuals to work with us to fund schools, liveli-hood training and safety monitoring to change the options available for children and their families.'

Farmer School

Bill Guyton is president of the World Cocoa Foundation, a body set up by chocolate manufacturers in 2000 to nurture the cocoa industry. He disagrees that nothing has been done. He says that a lot of effort has been put into the issue, and that African governments are taking it seriously. With a his-tory of NGO [non-governmental organization] work behind him, Guyton's views shouldn't be lightly dismissed, despite his role in the industry lobby group.

He believes that the foundation's Sustainable Tree Crops Program could influence cocoa farming from the ground up by teaching the farmers to work more intelligently—without

"Sweet, Sweet Denial," cartoon by Barry Deutsch, from amptoons.com. Reproduced by permission.

the need for legislation from above. Interestingly, his scheme isn't so different from Morley's requirements.

'We're trying to reach 150,000 farmers over the next five years in Ghana, Ivory Coast, Nigeria, Liberia and Cameroon', Guyton explains. 'We set up Farmer Field Schools and teach them how to manage their crops and their incomes better.

According to Global Exchange, a lobby group based in San Francisco, farmers typically earn between US $30 and US $100 a year for their entire crop.

'One of the most difficult things to teach farmers is pricing and the world market', he continues. 'Yet I was in Indonesia recently and was amazed to see how many of the farmers—miles from anywhere—had mobile phones and were keeping up to date. I'd like to see more African farmers empowered like that'.

Guyton points out that one of the major challenges in cocoa farming is that, often, one third of the crop is lost to diseases and pests. Farmers who attend the schools learn practices that don't require pesticides—such as pruning the trees, keeping the area beneath them clear and planting other crops nearby to naturally reduce the incidence of pests. They can also raise other topics such as child labour and health concerns about HIV/AIDS and malaria.

Farmers who have been to 'school' are showing a 25–55 per cent increase in income, which Guyton prefers to instituting a system of minimum price fixing, as favoured by Fairtrade. Either way, the low returns earned from cocoa play a huge part in the child labour problem. Many families are content for their young children to work with machetes in pesticide-ridden fields rather than attending school—simply because they are too poor and feel they have no choice than to do so.

The Price Is Wrong

The harsh truth for the world's cocoa farmers is that they are paid very little at the farm gate. While the price of their crop can fluctuate widely on the international market due to weather conditions and civil war, it's generally on an upward curve. According to Global Exchange, a lobby group based in San Francisco, farmers typically earn between US$30 and US$100 a year for their entire crop. The current market price is about US$2,370 per tonne. It takes about 100 beans to make a chocolate bar and, according to TransFair USA, the farmers earn approximately one cent for each 60-cent chocolate bar sold in the USA.

Farmers need to set their prices so that they can survive both bad harvests and civil unrest, but it's impossible for them to know that they should be charging more when global prices rise, as each farmer—from Belize to Vietnam—operates independently. The only solution is for the manufacturers to take an ethical stance, yet so far, only small Fairtrade outfits such as Divine and ChocAid are prepared to cooperate. Fairtrade principles include a fixed price for cocoa beans and a dividend from profits spent on local projects including housing and health care.

Nobody wants to have a guilty conscience eating chocolate.

Meanwhile, chocolate manufacturers claim that they can do little to help as they don't farm cocoa themselves, instead buying the beans through huge intermediary groups. No wonder raised eyebrows greeted the £20milllon [20 million British pounds] purchase of organic chocolate manufacturer Green & Black's, one of the most famous names in fair trade, by Cadbury Schweppes. In response to the news *Ethical Consumer* magazine dropped Green & Black's from third in its ethical chocolate league table to 12th.

Interestingly, while Cadbury still refuses to discuss the setting of fixed minimum prices, it has just launched its own £1million initiative, the Cadbury's Cocoa Partnership, which aims to improve farming conditions and also to encourage the next generation of farmers. This latter incentive is purely good business: Cadbury has identified that a 40 per cent fall in income among Ghanaian farmers is likely to lead to a slump in the number of farmers in the future.

Whatever the motivation, the scheme will bring huge social benefits with the building of schools, libraries and wells. James Boateng, managing director of Cadbury Ghana, says: 'I grew up on a cocoa farm, and owe my education to the prosperity that cocoa brought to my family. In Ghana, there is the phrase "*kookoo obatanpa*", which means "cocoa is a good parent; it looks after you". We hope that with this initiative, Cadbury and our partners can be a good parent to cocoa'.

Choosing Ethical Chocolate

Meanwhile, David Wilson, the managing director of Chocaid-.com—which only buys its beans from Fairtrade suppliers in the Dominican Republic and hands a share of its profits to Save the Children projects in Ethiopia—is sure he has made the soundest decision on his supply chain. 'This is not all about making masses of profit,' he says. 'I chose to produce ethical chocolate after hearing about the horrors of child labour in Ivory Coast. I realised that we could make a difference to people's lives if we all chose to buy fair-trade, ethical products. Of course, everyone wants to make a living, but you have to give something back'.

Wilson is investigating whether it's possible to grow cocoa in Ethiopia to help the communities further by giving them a new cash crop. 'I know that the living I am making isn't at the expense of other people's children,' he adds. 'And it's good for the consumers, too: nobody wants to have a guilty conscience eating chocolate'.

For Egyptian Children, Child Labor Is a Way of Life

Alaa Shahine

According to Alaa Shahine, for many Egyptian children, working is a way of life. In a country wracked by poverty, millions of children work to help support their families. Adults often take children out of school, worried that children will gain no vocational skills in the classroom. Child labor is socially accepted in Egypt, and in the case of many dysfunctional families, children suffer the consequences, ending up homeless and on the streets or working long hours for marginal pay. Alaa Shahine is a reporter who writes for Al Jazeera *and* Reuters.

As you read, consider the following questions:

1. How do many Egyptian families feel about children working at a young age?
2. According to children interviewed at a homeless shelter, how effective was their schooling?
3. According to Rami Salama, who supervises child workers, why is it necessary to employ children?

Mohamed Gad walks barefoot through the muddy tannery, seemingly not bothered by the acrid odours of chemicals and the stink of unprocessed skins.

Alaa Shahine, "Egyptian Children Trade Childhood for Money," Reuters, December 3, 2006. www.themercury.co.za. Reproduced by permission.

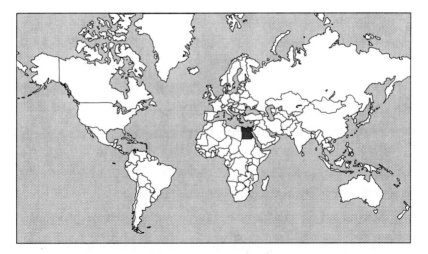

He places piles of shaved leather on a cart, pulls it across the workshop and unloads the lot next to the colouring drums where the leather is cleaned and tanned using chrome.

Tall and well-built, Gad joined the tannery just before he turned 15, after having worked in several menial jobs for four years after leaving school.

"The school was failing me every year and still charged me money, so I quit," he said while arranging the leather on the cart.

About 2.7 million children work in Egypt, or about 10% of the under-14 population.

"Now I want to learn this craft to make money out of it."

Helping Gad was Mohamed, who looked younger but was too shy to speak.

Children as Breadwinners

About 2.7 million children work in Egypt, or about 10% of the under-14 population, official figures show. The majority work in agriculture, mainly harvesting crops and hand-picking pests off cotton.

Hundreds of thousands of children, many of them homeless, also toil in menial jobs at tanneries and garages, or sell tissues and newspapers at traffic lights.

"There is abject poverty in Egypt, so families use children as breadwinners," said Nevine Osman, a child labour expert for the International Labour Organisation in Cairo.

Gad says he earns about 320 Egyptian pounds a month, more than some state employees. He sends half the money to his family in Assiut, a poor area in upper Egypt.

Mahmoud Mortada, who runs a non-government organisation helping children who work at pottery shops, said many families approved of children working.

"There is a social acceptance of child labour," he said. "People are unaware of the dangers of children working for more than 10 hours a day."

Gad's tannery is in Cairo's working class area of Magra al-Oyoun, where streams of sewage run along narrow, unpaved alleys and piles of animal waste are left to rot.

A Children's Homeless Shelter

At a shelter run by Hope Village, an Egyptian non-government organisation helping street children, 12-year-old Wagdy Abdel-Aziz said he was paid to roam the streets to collect plastic between dusk and dawn to avoid detection by the authorities.

The shelter hosts about 25 homeless children each day and offers them hot meals, showers and beds.

"I haven't got used to work, but it does not bother me anymore," said 13-year-old Ali Shabaan, who worked as a mechanic and a carpenter before his current job, which is to erect and furnish tents that are used for weddings and funerals.

After a meal of beans and cheese, he and the other children huddled in a small room watching cartoon movies on a

An Egyptian Boy Helps Support His Family

Nine-year-old Abdel Moti exemplifies the reasons why some very young children in Egypt end up working.

Abdel, the youngest child seen working at one brick factory near Arab Jbour, said he has worked at the plant since age 8, driving a donkey cart each day. He earns about $3.60 a day to help his mother, who works as a house maid. Often the money the boy makes goes to pay for medicines for his paralyzed father.

Abdel said he has no regrets about leaving school to work, because this way he can earn money.

Omar Sihan,
"Child Workers in Egypt a Growing Problem,"
Associated Press, 2008.

computer screen and playing cards, custom-made with drawings warning against the dangers of smoking, illegal drugs and HIV/AIDS.

"I haven't got used to work, but it does not bother me anymore," said 13-year-old Ali Shabaan.

Most children interviewed at the shelter said that they were illiterate despite having spent several years at school.

Families at Fault

The International Labour Organisation says that there are about 218 million child labourers and about 100 million legally-employed adolescent workers around the world. In some regions, the majority of those workers encountered some form of violence or abuse.

Domestic employees, young people working in the informal economy, modern forms of slavery and those doing dangerous work like mining or working on plantations are most at risk, the organisation says.

In Egypt many poor families take their children out of school, fearing that they will learn no skills in the classroom and will end up jobless after graduation. Experts say that the education system is failing to meet the needs of the labour market.

The government says that the unemployment rate stands at 9.5%, but the figure is widely believed to be much higher.

Gad's boss, Rami Salama, says that he cannot afford to have adults doing menial jobs. "If you look at China, it has flooded the world with its products because of the (cheap) labour cost," Salama said.

But the emotional cost to vulnerable children who are forced to work from an early age—and sometimes exposed to sexual assault and illegal drugs—is very high.

"Our parents are the reason behind this," [12-year-old Amal Shoukry] said, tears welling up in her eyes.

"They are also more prone to depression, anxiety and insomnia than normal children," said Shams Labib, a clinical psychologist with Doctors of the World, an international health and human rights organisation.

"They usually suffer from family problems. Those who should love and protect them abuse them," she said.

Amal Shoukry, a 12-year-old girl who has worked as a servant for half of her life, agrees. "Our parents are the reason behind this," she said, tears welling up in her eyes.

Periodical Bibliography

Marigee P. Bacolod and Priya Ranjan
"Why Children Work, Attend School, or Stay Idle: The Roles of Ability and Household Wealth," *Economic Development & Cultural Change*, July 2008.

Mita Bhattacharya
"Small Hands of Slavery: Mita Bhattacharya Looks at the Status of Child Labour in India in the Era of Trade Liberalisation," *Monash Business Review*, November 2007.

Deborah Dunn
"Is It Fair to Eat Chocolate?" *Slapping Stones*, November–December 2008.

Laura Lloyd
"'The Price of Sugar' Tells a Bitter Story," *National Catholic Reporter*, November 16, 2007.

Hannah Lobel
"Behind the Loom: The Rugmark Foundation Works to Keep Kids Out of the Rug Industry," *Utne Reader*, September–October 2006.

Reid Maki
"Children Work Long and Hard in America's Fields," *Faces: People, Places, and Cultures*, April 2006.

Christian Parenti
"Chocolate's Bittersweet Economy," *Fortune International* (Asia Edition), February 4, 2008.

Sadaf Qureshi
"Blood Chocolate: A Just Dessert?" *The Humanist*, September–October 2008.

Bruce Stokes
"When Childhood Is Denied," *National Journal*, June 28, 2008.

Salil Tripathi
"Child Labour: India's Small Workforce," *New Statesman*, vol. 136, December 3, 2007.

Michael Wines
"Africa Adds to Miserable Ranks of Child Workers," *New York Times*, August 24, 2006.

GLOBALVIEWPOINTS

CHAPTER 2

The Dangers of Child Labor

Kenyan Children Harvest Crops in Dangerous Conditions

Karen Fanning

In the following viewpoint, Karen Fanning writes that over a million former schoolchildren now work producing crops in Kenya, where a combination of dire events, including an economic downturn and the AIDS epidemic, has forced thousands of children out of school and into the fields. These jobs are dangerous, as children are overworked, underfed, and ill from exposure to pesticides. Injuries go untreated since medical care is virtually non-existent. Humanitarian organizations are trying to alleviate the suffering and get these children back to school where, Fanning suggests, they would prefer to be and where they belong. Karen Fanning is a contributing writer for Scholastic News Online.

As you read, consider the following questions:

1. According to the article, about how many child laborers are there in Kenya?
2. What is the percentage decrease in enrollments in Kenyan schools over the last two decades?
3. How are humanitarian organizations trying to support Kenyan schools?

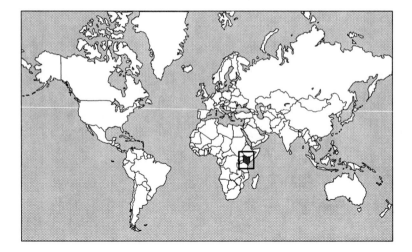

When Martha Wamboi's father died four years ago, her mother was left to care for six children alone. Martha was soon forced to drop out of school to help support the family. Now, the 13-year-old rises before dawn to work, barefoot, in the vast coffee fields of Kenya.

"I don't want to go picking coffee," says Martha, as she lugs a large metal container of coffee beans up a long ramp. "I want to go back to school."

Martha is just one of an estimated 4 million child laborers in Kenya. Instead of attending school, these children work for pennies an hour, day in and day out.

More than one million young people work in agriculture—harvesting coffee, tea, and other crops. At night, they go home to small, rundown houses clustered along dirt roads.

"There is trash everywhere," says Len Morris, a documentary filmmaker who has spent the past two years filming child labor across the globe. "There are no public services, so the trash has to be burned." And because there are no plumbing facilities, waste water runs in streams through the villages.

The Price of an Education

Most Kenyans live on less than a dollar a day. So it is not surprising that many children are working instead of attending school.

"Over 60 percent of the population lives below the poverty line," says Peter Munene, a social worker in Nairobi. "Now what would be the alternative for such a family? To take the child out of school, or to do without a meal?"

Too often, though, farm owners take advantage of struggling families. "Children become a very good source of labor because they are cheap and can work long hours," says Wangari Maathai, founder of the Green Belt Movement, an environmental group. Owners "will overwork them, underfeed them, and overexpose them to pesticides."

Still, most parents view education as the only way to free their children from the poverty that has gripped families for generations.

"Children become a very good source of labor because they are cheap and can work long hours. . . . [Owners] will overwork them, underfeed them, and overexpose them to pesticides."

"Very many families have gone to great pains to have their children educated," says Munene. "Some have even sold their own pieces of land. Parents have had to sell everything they had, and remain with nothing, just to have their children back in school."

For families like Martha's, the cost of education is simply too great. But it hasn't always been that way.

Schools in Kenya were free until 1982, when the government cut spending on education. The nation had to pay debts it owed to the World Bank and the International Monetary Fund. Since then, the cost of education has been shared by parents.

Millions of Children Working on Farms

Seventy per cent of working children are in agriculture—over 132 million girls and boys aged 5–14 years old. The vast majority of the world's child labourers are not toiling in factories and sweatshops or working as domestics or street vendors in urban areas, they are working on farms and plantations, often from sun up to sun down, planting and harvesting crops, spraying pesticides, and tending livestock on rural farms and plantations. These children play an important role in crop and livestock production, helping supply some of the food and drink we consume, and the fibres and raw materials we use to make other products.

International Programme on the Elimination of Child Labour (IPEC), "Agriculture," www.ilo.org.

While the government pays teacher salaries, parents must pay for their children's books, school supplies, exam fees, tuition fees, uniforms, and extracurricular activities. With so many parents unable to pay, school enrollment rates have plummeted (dropped sharply) over the last two decades—from nearly 90 percent to less than 50 percent in some regions.

The AIDS epidemic (outbreak) has also reduced enrollment. The deadly disease has left roughly one million children without parents. Many of these orphans have quit school to support their younger siblings.

The Danger of Pesticides

Kenya's farmland has been green and lush for centuries. But neglect, erosion, and pesticides (harmful chemicals) have devastated many fields.

There is no drinking water for children working in the fields, other than what they collect from irrigation ditches. That water contains pesticides.

"Your hands [hurt from] the chemicals that are applied. They also burn your face. It's as if hot water has been poured on your face."

Benta Adera is all too familiar with the toxic (poisonous) chemicals that are sprayed on crops to keep bugs away. On Saturdays, when she is not in school, Benta reports to the coffee fields by 7 a.m. She earns less than a dollar for 10 hours of work.

"It's not good," says Benta, a fifth-grader at the Kia-ora Primary School, which is about an hour outside of Nairobi, Kenya's capital. "Your hands [hurt from] the chemicals that are applied. They also burn your face. It's as if hot water has been poured on your face."

"Eyes get poked, legs get cut, arms get scraped," says filmmaker Len Morris. "There is no medical care. There are no doctors. If a child is injured, he or she is left to suffer."

Pesticides are not the only hazard (danger) for coffee pickers. Snake bites, back strain, and other injuries go with the job.

"Eyes get poked, legs get cut, arms get scraped," says filmmaker Len Morris. "There is no medical care. There are no doctors. If a child is injured, he or she is left to suffer."

A Helping Hand

Today, humanitarian organizations are teaming up with teachers, students, and parents to raise money for Kenya's schools.

An elementary school in the Thika District harvests honey, beans, and corn, which it sells to local growers and villagers. The proceeds will pay for the education of 40 students.

Similarly, the Ngegu Primary School in the Kiambu District has grown napier grass, which local farmers use to feed their cows. Sales from the grass have helped pay for students' uniforms and books.

Thanks to income-generating projects such as these, children like Benta can attend school.

"I love geography, science, and math," says the 12-year-old. "I've never missed school. After you get educated, you get a good job instead of picking coffee."

Long after Benta has returned home from school, Martha is still sorting through coffee beans. When her workday finally ends, she leaves with just 60 shillings—less than a dollar. She spends 10 shillings on a piece of sugarcane and a doughnut. The rest she will give to her mother.

Martha hopes to leave the coffee fields for good someday and return to school. But for now, she must work.

"I stopped going to school because of money," she says. "I want to go back to school. I'd like to be a nurse."

In Southeast Asia and Elsewhere, Child Sex Tourism Is a Significant Problem

Natalie Ann McCauley

In the following viewpoint, Natalie Ann McCauley explains that child sex tourism is a growing global industry in which poverty-stricken children are subjected to a life of prostitution, serving adults who travel to foreign countries for the purpose of engaging in illicit sexual conduct with juveniles. Child sex trafficking is a dangerous form of slavery that can lead children to suffer lifelong emotional and physical debilitation, McCauley asserts. Children have the right to be safe from sexual abuse, McCauley states, and countries are banding together to prosecute adults who facilitate or solicit illegal sexual activity. Natalie Ann Mc-Cauley wrote this report for Child Wise, a child protection charity working in Australia, and throughout Asia and the Pacific.

As you read, consider the following questions:

1. According to the article, how do child sex offenders avoid getting caught?
2. How many children are trafficked across the globe every year, according to the author?
3. What diseases are common among children who are trafficked for sexual purposes?

Natalie Ann McCauley, *Traffic Jam: A Report on the Commercial Sexual Exploitation of Children*, South Melbourne, Australia: Child Wise, 2004. Copyright © 2004 Child Wise. Reproduced by permission.

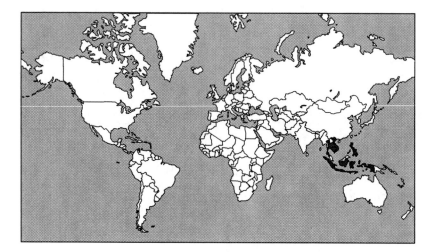

I came here looking for work. My family sent me. We needed money ... People were saying many foreigners come here and there was lots of work. Not long after arriving the man that owned the guest house I worked at sold me to an American for 3 days ... he said he was good customer, came every year and I should do whatever he wanted. That's how I started ...

—Chai, 15 year old boy Jomtien beach, Thailand

The sexual exploitation, abuse and prostitution of children is a global problem. Over the past 30 years this sexual exploitation has developed into a flourishing child sex tourism industry with thousands of Australians travelling overseas to abuse children every year. Australian sex tourists have been identified in over 20 countries but all countries in the world can be implicated in the child sex tourism industry.

A Horrific Industry

Millions of children around the world are involved in prostitution and child sex tourism. Much of the demand comes from local men but there is an increasing demand from foreigners coming to destinations for the purpose of abusing children. Children are trafficked internally and across borders to accommodate the high demand for child prostitutes in certain tourism destinations.

Reports in the 1980s [told] of the horrific brothel fire in Bangkok where 5 children were found dead chained to beds and the 11 year old girl in the Philippines who died after an Austrian tourist abused her and left a broken vibrator inside her body. These stories brought the enormity of the child sexual exploitation problem in our region to our attention, but these violations are still happening and they have yet to be stopped.

Child sex tourism can happen anywhere but child sex offenders will go to destinations where they think they will not get caught. They will avoid places where law enforcement is high and children are protected. Many children involved in the child sex industry come from vulnerable backgrounds of poverty, low levels of education or no education, broken families or no family, ethnic minorities and lack of citizenship.

Globalisation is assisting the [child sex] offenders especially with the wide use of the Internet. They communicate quickly and inform the networks of offenders where to go and what they will get when they arrive.

Globalisation is assisting the offenders especially with the wide use of the Internet. They communicate quickly and inform the networks of offenders where to go and what they will get when they arrive. Travel has become significantly cheaper and communities far more vulnerable. Globalisation and increased consumerism has assisted with the supply of children, the ease in transporting children across the globe and within a country, as well, the demand for goods and increased wealth have assisted the persuasiveness of the procurers.

Children in this horrific industry are a major reason for the increase in HIV/AIDS cases in children throughout SE [Southeast] Asia. They are particularly susceptible to physical, psychological and social damage. Child sexual exploitation destroys communities and tourism destinations.

Co-ordinated regional action to enforce the rights of children and prosecute the criminals involved is needed to prevent this horrible trade.

The Garbage in Manila

Walking through the slum area it was like any other slum area except that this one had a bit more space on the paths that weave in and out like a maze. I was being taken to the area where many of the 250,000 Filipino children in prostitution originate—a massive rubbish dump on the outskirts of Manila.

You smell it before you see it. The slum area engulfs you so it is some time before you catch a glimpse. I caught a glimpse from the corner of my eye and it took my breath away—Could that be it? Don't let that be it. It's huge!

On the steep hill made of compressed garbage we climbed up to the edge of the cliff of garbage, I lost my breath. The enormity of the mountain of rubbish astounded me. It didn't seem real. It is easily 150 metres in height and it is approximately 1km [kilometre] in circumference. The smell could knock you down if the heat from the rubbish and poisons going into your skin didn't hurt so much.

It is an incomprehensible sight to see thousands of people and hundreds of children working and living on this man made mountain. The demand for children in the Philippines is huge. With an estimated 300,000 Japanese men making the journey to the Philippines every year to abuse children, the challenge is to keep up the supply of children.

My first daughter was sold last year to a man who will give her work, schooling and money. What can I give my children? It is better if they are not here ...

—A mother with 2 more girls, working on the dump

The realities of this dump sight are confronting. This community works together, they have ropes and lines erected for easy access of rubbish from the top of the mountain, down to those packing at the middle. They work around the clock and everyone, including the children, [is] involved.

We get 1 peso for a cube of packed paper that takes 2 weeks to collect. If we are lucky we collect enough rubbish to make 22 peso over 2 weeks. We need this ... a bag (1kg [kilogram]) of rice is 21 peso.

—A mother with 1 girl and 2 boys, working on the dump

None of the children are in school but the atmosphere and love of the community here is wonderful. The children have put together a soccer ball made out of rubbish and we all play a world cup match on the top of the dump.... It was much like any childhood game, a lot was at stake. There was a lot of laughter and smiles despite the situation they were in, but it was hard to think that most of these children are headed for a darker life one day soon.

They come here every few weeks when they need more workers. Good opportunities for them, and it helps the ones left behind.

—A father with 5 girls, 2 already sold, working on the dump

The generosity and smiles were endless. The families we talked to were shocked that the work opportunities were not what they thought. They love their children and families— they just want something better for their children.

The Trafficking of Children

I came to Manila 5 years ago, I was 10. I was brought here from East Java (Indonesia) by ship to work in a factory with 4 other children from my community. They promised my family they would take care of me . . . they promised. I worked in a karaoke bar in Quezon City (Manila) as a prostitute for 4 years before I escaped. I don't know where the others are . . .

—*Nong, 15 year old girl, Manila, the Philippines, 2003*

Nong is one of the estimated 1.2 million children trafficked across the globe every year.

The trafficking of children is a global problem. It is a multi-billion dollar industry that is growing at an alarming rate. The statistics are daunting, but it is important to remember that within these large overwhelming numbers we are talking about a child, a single child at risk.

'People trafficking' is not a new phenomenon. This industry has a long history dating back to the dawn of civilization and early forms of slavery. Modern 'people trafficking' has, however, escalated over the last 20 years, and today it would be hard to find a country that is not involved in this industry either as a sending country, a transit country or a receiving country.

Children are particularly vulnerable to trafficking and despite a number of international conventions over the past 15 years—including the UN [United Nations] Convention on the Rights of the Child (UNCRC), 1989—this hideous trade still exists and is escalating.

'People trafficking' is not a new phenomenon. This industry has a long history dating back to the dawn of civilization and early forms of slavery.

The region of SE Asia and the Pacific now accounts for nearly 50% of the child trade. Throughout this region there are many factors over the last 40 years that have contributed to this increasing business in the region including military, political, economic and social factors.

The Viet Nam War in the 60s and 70s, and the United Nations Transitional Authority of Cambodia (UNTAC) in the 90s

What Can You Do?

Child sex tourism is a serious violation of children's rights. Whether you are a traveller, tourist, tourism professional or simply a concerned individual, there are steps you can take to combat commercial sexual exploitation of children in tourism.

1. Choose travel and tourism companies that have a policy against child sex tourism, such as those that have signed and implemented the Code of Conduct.

2. If your regular travel agents or tour operators do not have such a policy, encourage them to develop one.

3. Consult the ECPAT Web site to find out more about the situation of children in certain tourism destinations.

4. Speak out against child sex tourism to your peers.

5. Contribute to local organisations working against commercial sexual exploitation of children.

6. When travelling, do not hesitate to report any suspicion of sexual exploitation to local authorities (a list of hotlines is available at www.unwto.org/protect_child ren/). If this is not possible, please report to a local NGO [non-governmental organisation] or to ECPAT [End Child Prostitution, Child Pornography, and Trafficking of Children for Sexual Purposes] International.

ECPAT International, Combating Child Sex Tourism: Questions and Answers, *2008. www.ecpat.net.*

were both major sources of the demand for the sex industry throughout SE Asia over the past 40 years. The increased military presence in the region gave way to a booming sex industry and a massive trafficking trade in women and children.

During the 80s there was also a mass shift from the centrally planned economies of the past to market-orientated economies. This dramatic shift created opportunities for high-level corruption in the vulnerable countries of SE Asia. These new market systems also placed Viet Nam, Cambodia and Lao PDR [People's Democratic Republic] into a depression of high poverty, high unemployment and mass inequity. The 1997 Asian Economic Crisis also created a perfect environment for the child trade to flourish.

> We had no money, no food, it is my place to help provide for my family. So when they came to offer me work, good work, factory work . . . what could I do but say yes. It is the right thing to do. But this work is not the right thing to do . . . I will never pay them back.
>
> —*Tui, 13 years, Child Prostitute, Phnom Penh*
> *Trafficked from Viet Nam to Cambodia*

Modern Slavery

The sex trafficking industry is fuelled by poverty, lack of education, unemployment and lack of opportunities, weak law enforcement, globalisation, the lure of easy money, the profitability of the trade, [and] Internet pornography, and the spread of HIV/AIDS has increased the demand for younger and younger girls.

The United Nations' Protocol to Prevent, Suppress and Punish Trafficking in Persons, Especially Women and Children provides us with a universally accepted definition of trafficking;

> 'Trafficking in persons' shall mean the recruitment, transportation, transfer, harbouring or receipt of persons, by means of the threat or use of force or other forms of coercion, of abduction, or fraud, or deception, of abuse of power or of a position of vulnerability or of giving or receiving of payments having control over another person, for the purpose of exploitation. Exploitation shall include, at the minimum, the exploitation or the prostitution of others or other forms of sexual exploitation, forced labour or services, slavery or practices similar to slavery, servitude or the removal of organs.

This protocol also states that the consent of a person under the age of 18 does not de-criminalise the act of trafficking.

The consent of a person under the age of 18 does not decriminalise the act of trafficking.

There are two types of trafficking: internal trafficking and cross-border trafficking. Many children are brought into the major cities of this region to work as prostitutes and beggars. The beggar children of major cities are particularly vulnerable to child sexual exploitation and further trafficking across borders.

Cross-border trafficking involves children being taken from their home countries into new areas. This may be done by force, they may be sold or they may leave willingly in the hope of a new and improved life. In 2003 two children were found in a crate, in cargo, on a transport ship. They had been sold by their families in Indonesia and were headed for the sex tourism industry of Thailand when they were found, drugged, in a ship stopover in Malaysia.

The large trafficking syndicates across the globe are very powerful. This trade in people ranks third of the biggest trades in the world behind the arms trade and drug trade. It is believed that many of the people involved in this trade are also involved in other major transnational crimes.

The children exposed to this type of slavery are subject to much physical abuse. They are exposed to sexually transmitted diseases such as HIV/AIDS, syphilis, herpes and urinary tract infections. Many are left with permanent physical damage to their reproductive organs. The extreme isolation, beatings, rape, imprisonment and constant mental abuse leaves the children broken, with little hope.

After much criticism over the past 10 years, many governments are now trying to combat this harsh form of modern slavery.

They sold my village a new village house. Well ... they offered the house and said if my sister and I come and work for them we could pay it off. They would give us schooling as well as jobs. That was 6 years ago and we have not gone to school.

—16 year old boy,
working as a prostitute in Phnom Penh, Cambodia

Extraterritorial Legislation

"Thai guy, young, fit, hunk, caring and English speaking, would like to be your personal guide when in Thailand. Prefer older men. Contact my friend in Perth."

This advertisement in a Perth [Australia] community newspaper led to the arrest, in 2003, of former private school teacher John Joseph Kosky, on charges of attempting to lure prospective child sex tourists in Thailand. This ad is in the code language used by paedophiles, and generated thousands of calls to the retirement village where Kosky lived.

It is an offence in many countries to commit crimes against children overseas. These laws are called extraterritorial legislation—and they are proving to be quite powerful in the fight against child sex tourism.

There are now over 30 countries that have these laws which gives a sending country the capacity to prosecute their citizens and residents for a crime that they committed away from home. Some of the countries include Australia, Austria, Belgium, Canada, China, Denmark, Finland, France, Germany, Ireland, Italy, Japan, Luxembourg, the Netherlands, New Zealand, Norway, Portugal, Spain, Sweden, Switzerland, Taiwan, Thailand, the UK, and the USA.

Most countries and specifically the countries of SE Asia have their own legislation to protect children from exploitation and abuse. It is important to remember that where an offence is committed locally by a foreigner and the offender(s) is apprehended in the country in which the offence is committed, he/she should be charged under local legislation.

There have been 16 prosecutions under the Australian Crimes (Child Sex Tourism) Act, 1994. It is very difficult to prosecute under the Crimes (Child Sex Tourism) Act 1994. There are many restrictions regarding the collection of evidence, reporting procedures and transnational agreements. This is being overcome by further training in Embassies, communities and with the work of the Australian Federal Police on the ground. . . .

A Child's Right to Be Safe in This World

He organises all of us through the older boys. There must be five boys at his door every night when he gets home from work. One boy refused one evening and he was stabbed later that night by one of the leaders. No one has refused since. I am one of the lucky ones as he pays for a room for me and buys me food and clothes.

—*14 year old street kid, Hanoi, Viet Nam,*
talking about an expatriate business man

Children are entitled to all the rights guaranteed by the Universal Declaration of Human Rights but they also need special protection and care. The United Nations Convention on the Rights of the Child (UNCRC) is the most widely accepted human rights treaty in the world. The convention's objective is to protect children from discrimination, neglect and abuse.

Several of the 54 articles of the convention, which was approved in 1989, refer to sexual exploitation and its consequences. These require that countries that have ratified the convention take appropriate action to protect children from: "all forms of physical or mental violence, injury or abuse, including sexual abuse" by parent(s), guardian(s) or caretaker (Article 19); from the "inducement or coercion of a child to engage in any unlawful sexual activity"; from "the exploitative use of children in prostitution or other unlawful sexual practices"; from "the exploitative use of children in pornographic performances or materials" (Article 34) and from "the abduction of, sale of, or traffic in children for any purpose" (Article 35).

It is our responsibility to take 'appropriate action' to protect children no matter where they are in the world. It is important to remember that many of the factors that lead children to be vulnerable to all forms of exploitation are also violations of human rights including the right to education, shelter and food. The basics of life.

During a trip to Bali, Indonesia (Jan 2004) a conversation was had with a 16 year boy. It was clear that abuse was happening within some communities by expatriates [those who live in a country other than their own] that were 'sponsoring' communities that are quite destitute. These expatriates supply food, where there was none; shelter, where there was none; education, where there was no opportunity; and trauma through sexual abuse and manipulation.

Q: Is it a price worth paying?

A: [With a long pause and deep thought . . .]

That is very hard to answer . . .

The sacrifice of this young man for his family and community. The burden at such a young age. No child should ever have to answer that question . . . No children should have to shoulder such burden and pain. No child should have to sacrifice their future and happiness for their families and community. The communities should never be left that vulnerable.

Colombia's Girl Prostitutes Must Be Removed from Danger

Drea Knufken

Colombia is a country with a robust economy and, according to Drea Knufken in the following viewpoint, a thriving market for young female prostitutes. Over a million young girls earn a living in the sex trade in Colombia, states Knufken, and these girls need to be protected. Various international and Colombian agencies are trying to save as many girls as possible from their dangerous and degrading work. The Colombian government has not always been helpful, Knufken claims, and is sometimes antagonistic toward the very girls who most need help, yet government agencies and non-governmental organizations continue to protect child prostitutes through a wide range of services. Drea Knufken is a writer interested in women's issues. She also specializes in articles about food, health, travel, and the outdoors.

As you read, consider the following questions:

1. How does Knufken show Colombia to be a country of contrasts?
2. According to Knufken, why do Colombian girls become prostitutes?
3. What does the Renacer Institute do?

Drea Knufken, "A Child in Danger Is a Child That Cannot Wait—Colombia and Child Prostitution in Today's World," *Women News Network–WNN*, September 16, 2007. Reproduced by permission.

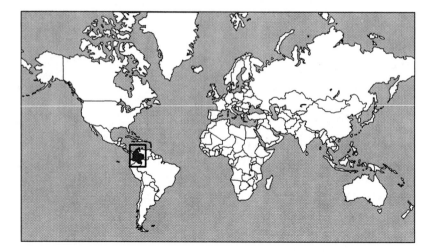

Colombia is a land of contrasts, as anyone who's read [writer and Nobel laureate] Gabriel Garcia Marquez can attest. It is [a large] country in South America, with a 2005 population of 45.6 million, and known for its rich economic resources and its guerilla fighters, its natural beauty and its syndicated crime, its high-quality heart surgeons and its drug traffickers. The economy is doing well under the leadership of President Alvaro Uribe, and, as of 2000, it was home to two thirds of the world's kidnappings.

A Huge Hidden Industry

A volatile country, if anything. A colorful country. Colombia is attracting increasing numbers of tourists as well, as the World Tourism Organization, which is having its November 2007 conference in Colombia, can attest. And underneath it all, in the shadows of the cartels, the syndicates, the beauty and the wars, are more than 1 million girl-children earning a living by selling their bodies.

Children become prostitutes for a variety of reasons. Poverty is often at the core: families prostitute out their girls in order to have enough income to survive; others sell their children to brothels and trade networks for the same reason.

Other children independently flee abusive domestic situations for the promise of a better life and find themselves in the sex industry; still others were soldiers or otherwise affected by one of Colombia's wars and, now displaced, find themselves with few options for surviving. Still others are kidnapped, or refugees from other regions.

In the shadows of the cartels, the syndicates, the beauty and the wars, are more than 1 million girl-children earning a living by selling their bodies.

Prostitution takes on different guises here. Some children end up in local brothels; others are placed into regional and international prostitution trade networks. These networks are often run by bigger syndicates also involved in narcotics, weapons, and counterfeiting. Children may be traded to neighboring countries like Venezuela, or to markets in countries as distant as Spain or Germany.

Children Need to Be Protected

Whether instigated by adverse conditions at home or involuntary actions, child prostitution in Colombia is as insidious as it is widespread. Colombia is known as a human supply company for prostitution networks abroad, the country itself is a known sex tourism destination, and prostitution is firmly embedded into the economy as a means of making a decent living wage. Still, as the United Nations Convention on the Rights of the Child, the CRC, which Colombia signed and ratified in 1989 and entered into force Sept. 2, 1990, suggests, children need to be protected. This is not only for their own well-being—child prostitution is correlated with illness, infertility, post-traumatic stress disorders, homelessness, and other afflictions—but for the good of the entire society.

While the U.S. government helped to write sections of the CRC, [as of 2007] the U.S. Senate has still not completely rati-

Child Prostitution in Greece

On the day her life changed, when she was 13 years old, Majlinda was on the way to help her aunt with the ironing of clothes in preparation for her cousin's wedding in their village in northern Albania. She was a little short of reaching the house when three strange men stopped her. They grabbed her, bundled her into a car, blindfolded, bound and gagged her; she was then driven to the southern town of Gjirokastra. Not until the men and Majlinda had crossed the border with Greece and reached Corinth was she told: 'Now you are going to work.'

Ed Vulliamy, "Streets of Despair,"
The Observer *(London), October 3, 2004.*

fied the international treaty on the Rights of the Child because of ongoing contentions concerning sections of the Convention which prevent jurisprudence and sentencing against children under the age of 18. Currently inside the United States, numerous separate states continue today to charge and sentence children under the age of 18, which clearly goes against tenets of the treaty itself, leaving the U.S. laws far behind and outside the guidelines and jurisdictions of the CRC.

The Colombian government, in contrast, seems publicly to realize a greater need for the guidelines provided by the CRC. National Police have rounded up child prostitutes on several occasions and brought them to the Renacer Institute, a nonprofit organization which offers child prostitutes room, board, and education in exchange for a promise to stop working. Established as a nonprofit in 1994, the foundation has two houses that can support around 60 children. The *Colombia Journal* cites the example of Carolina and her sister, who ran away from their impoverished Bogota neighborhood in their mid-teens in order to escape familial abuse. It wasn't long before the two girls were working the streets of Bogota, making an income as prostitutes. Several months later, they were rounded up by police and taken to Renacer. The National Police also run "Colombia Without Prostitution," a prevention program aimed at preventing child prostitution through community and family education. The government has also collaborated with various NGOs [non-governmental organizations] to create a Plan of Action on Child Sexual Abuse in relation to its signing of the Convention of the Rights of the Child.

Much Work to Be Done

That said, the government's role though has been unpredictable, fluctuating between support of the children, neutrality, and enmity. According to Human Rights Watch, police have periodically been suspected of waging war on street children rather than helping them, sometimes even shooting them on the streets. The government is also a major donor to Renacer, but has significantly cut funds in the past.

> The government's role . . . has been unpredictable, fluctuating between support of the children, neutrality, and enmity. . . . Police have periodically been suspected of waging war on street children rather than helping them.

Despite difficulties, Renacer continues to be devoted to the cause of getting child prostitutes off the streets. Stella Cardenas Ovalle, Founding Member and Director of the Renacer Foundation, has, since 2001, been working hard to influence government policy and to steady law enforcement policies. Ovalle is building a long-term alliance of child protection organizations, like Renacer, that are only now beginning to network together. Using the power of numbers and statistics, the network will keep legal policy informed and work steadily to stimulate public awareness. The alliance will, if Ovalle's projections prove correct, be today's "most powerful catalyzing agent in the fight against commercial exploitation of children."

So far, the Fundacion Renacer has worked with ECPAT International (End Child Prostitution, Child Pornography and Trafficking of Children for Sexual Purposes), the Bogota District Council for the Comprehensive Care of Child Victims of Abuse and Sexual Exploitation, UNICEF [United Nations Children's Fund], and many other organizations. Internally, together, they protect child prostitutes through programs ranging from vocational education to psychotherapy, with the ultimate goal of helping them lead relatively settled lives in society.

Still, there remains much work to be done, especially in light of the complexity of the situation.

Where There Is War, There Are Child Soldiers

Coalition to Stop the Use of Child Soldiers

According to the Coalition to Stop the Use of Child Soldiers, the issue of children in combat continues to be a significant problem worldwide. While it may seem that the number of child soldiers is falling, in actuality, this may be due to fewer conflicts rather than a shift in policies regarding the use of young people in armed combat. Efforts to reduce the ranks of child soldiers have made little progress due to complex underlying problems that cannot be easily solved. Any time a conflict breaks out around the world, it is a safe assumption that child soldiers will be used, the coalition asserts. Until attitudes change so that governments and organizations value children, young people will continue to be used and abused in combat. The Coalition to Stop the Use of Child Soldiers is a London-based organization that documents and opposes child soldiering on a global scale. The organization works to prevent the recruitment and use of children as soldiers, to aid in their demobilization, and to facilitate their rehabilitation and reintegration into society.

As you read, consider the following questions:

1. According to the authors, armed groups in what countries have been charged with war crimes related to child soldiers by the International Criminal Court?

Coalition to Stop the Use of Child Soldiers, "Introduction," *Child Soldiers: Global Report 2008*, London, UK: Coalition to Stop the Use of Child Soldiers, 2008, pp. 12–16. Copyright © Coalition to Stop the Use of Child Soldiers. Reproduced by permission.

2. According to the Coalition to Stop the Use of Child Soldiers, how many countries used children in combat between April 2004 and October 2007?

3. What are the particular difficulties facing girl soldiers in terms of demobilization and reintegration programs?

Four years is a long time in a child's life. Much can happen that will touch the rest of their lives for good or for ill. Some children may live their lives in situations of peace and security. For countless others war continues to be all too real. Over this aspect of the adult world they have little say and no control.

Four years is sufficient for substantial developments in the life of a global movement. The last *Global Report* was published by the Coalition to Stop the Use of Child Soldiers in November 2004; since then [until 2008] the movement to end the use of child soldiers has seen continued progress towards a universal consensus against their use in hostilities, witnessed by the fact that over three-quarters of states have now signed, ratified or acceded to the Optional Protocol to the Convention on the Rights of the Child [an anti-child soldier accord] on the involvement of children in armed conflict.

The military recruitment of children ... and their use in hostilities is a ... phenomenon that still takes place in one form or another in at least 86 countries and territories worldwide.

Still Too Many Child Soldiers

On the ground, the consensus would appear to be reflected most clearly by a decrease in the number of conflicts in which children are directly involved—from 27 in 2004 to 17 by the end of 2007. The Coalition's research for this *Global Report* shows, however, that this downward trend is more the result of conflicts ending than the impact of initiatives to end child soldier recruitment and use. Indeed, where armed conflict does exist, child soldiers will almost certainly be involved. The majority of these children are in non-state armed groups, but the record of some governments is also little improved.

The figures for conflict do not reveal the whole picture. The military recruitment of children (under-18s) and their use in hostilities is a much larger phenomenon, that still takes place in one form or another in at least 86 countries and territories worldwide. This includes unlawful recruitment by armed groups, forcible recruitment by government forces, recruitment or use of children into militias or other groups associated with armed forces, their use as spies, as well as legal recruitment into peacetime armies.

The first important steps towards establishing individual criminal responsibility for those who recruit and use children in hostilities have been taken.

A Complex Solution

The findings make it clear that, despite the high level of international attention on the issue, the impact of that attention is yet to be felt by many children who are, or are at risk of becoming, child soldiers. They have reinforced the fact that a complex range of co-ordinated responses by multiple actors are required to achieve the goal of preventing children's involvement in armed conflict, obtaining their release and supporting successful reintegration. This will involve a more explicit recognition of child soldiers on the agendas of those involved in a whole range of initiatives, from conflict prevention, peacemaking and mediation through to peace-building and longer-term development.

Ultimately, if, over the next four years, the international community is to make good its promise to protect children from military exploitation, the level of political will, the amount of human and financial resources, the adherence to established best practice and the quantity as well as the quality of collaborative effort and imaginative endeavour must all be multiplied.

International Efforts Continue

The international framework to protect children from involvement in armed forces and groups has been reinforced and efforts have focused increasingly on field-level implementation.

The first important steps towards establishing individual criminal responsibility for those who recruit and use children in hostilities have been taken. War crimes charges relating to the conscription [forced enlistment], enlistment and active participation in hostilities of children under 15 years old have been issued by the International Criminal Court (ICC) against members of armed groups in the Democratic Republic of the Congo (DRC) and Uganda. A landmark in international justice was forged by the conviction in 2007 by the Special Court for Sierra Leone of four people on charges that included the recruitment and use of children during the civil war. The pursuit of justice has also been furthered by the work of truth commissions in Sierra Leone, Timor-Leste and recently Liberia, all of which have addressed the issue of child soldiers.

The Optional Protocol to the Convention on the Rights of the Child on the involvement of children in armed conflict (Optional Protocol)—the most specific prohibition of child soldiers under international law—has [as of 2008] been ratified by 120 states, up from 77 in mid-2004. The United Nations (UN) Committee on the Rights of the Child began to examine state party reports on the Optional Protocol implementation in January 2005. Their concluding observations are generating an increased momentum towards developing modalities for protecting children from military recruitment and use, as well as providing an insight into further measures that many governments must take if they are to achieve this goal.

Documenting Abuse

Building on previous actions, the UN Security Council adopted resolutions 1539 (2004) and 1612 (2005) calling for the establishment of a monitoring and reporting mechanism on children and armed conflict. Now set up in around a dozen countries, the mechanism is tasked with documenting six categories of grave abuse against children, including recruitment and use of child soldiers, in the situations of armed conflict listed in the annexes of the UN Secretary-General's regular reports on the topic. A Security Council working group on children and armed conflict was set up in 2005 to review reports submitted under the mechanism and to monitor progress in the development and implementation of time-bound action plans by warring parties to end their recruitment and use of child soldiers. The working group has issued conclusions based on the reports, transmitted letters and appeals to parties engaged in violations, and taken a range of other actions on situations where abuses against children have been committed.

The first actions by the Security Council to apply targeted measures against individuals specifically for recruiting and using children were taken in 2006, when a travel ban was imposed on an armed group leader in Côte d'Ivoire. A Security Council resolution the same year sought to subject to travel bans and asset freezing leaders in the DRC who recruited or used child soldiers.

Regional bodies have also continued to focus attention on this issue. The European Union's (EU) 2003 Guidelines on children and armed conflict were given practical direction by an implementation strategy issued in 2006. The same year a checklist on integration and protection of children was adopted to ensure that child rights and protection concerns are systematically addressed in European Security and Defence

Goverments That Used Child Soldiers in Armed Conflict, April 2004–October 2007

Israel

Chad

Myanmar

Yemen

Somalia

Democratic
Republic of the
Congo (DRC)

Sudan &
Southern
Sudan

Uganda

TAKEN FROM: Coalition to Stop the Use of Child Soliders, *Child Soliders: Global Report 2008*. London: Bell and Bain, 2008.

Policy (ESDP) operations and mission planning. The African Union (AU) renewed its calls for its member states to ratify the African Charter on the Rights and Welfare of the Child by the end of 2008 and to enact relevant implementing legislation by 2010. The Charter requires state parties *inter alia* [among other things] to refrain from recruiting children and to ensure that they do not take direct part in hostilities.

Major New Initiatives Against Child Soldiering

On the ground, tens of thousands of child soldiers have been released from armies and armed groups since 2004 as long-running conflicts in sub-Saharan Africa have ended. A major initiative to gather and compile accumulated experience from the demobilization [discharge of soldiers from combat] disarmament and reintegration (DDR) of child soldiers around the world culminated in the Paris Principles and Guidelines on children associated with armed forces or armed groups (Paris Principles). Endorsed by 66 governments at ministerial meetings in February and October in 2007, including many from conflict-affected countries, the Paris Principles offer guidance on protecting children from recruitment and on providing effective assistance to those already involved with armed groups or forces.

The large-scale recruitment and deployment of children by government forces in countries such as Burundi, Côte d'Ivoire, Guinea and Liberia ceased with the end of conflicts. More than half of countries worldwide have set the minimum age at which an individual can enter the military, including for training, at 18.

In response to international pressure and local initiatives, several armed groups have committed themselves to ending the recruitment and use of children. Groups in Côte d'Ivoire and Sri Lanka are working with the UN to develop and implement time-bound action plans to release children and prevent their recruitment. Ethnic armed groups in Myanmar have agreed to do likewise.

Real Protection Requires Redoubling of Effort

While the general direction is positive, the pace of progress is slow and its impact is not yet felt by the tens of thousands of children in the ranks of fighting forces. The international framework offers little real protection for countless others who are at risk of recruitment and use in conflict.

The Coalition has documented information on 21 countries or territories where children were deployed to areas of conflict between April 2004 and October 2007. Within this period conflicts ended in two of the 21—Indonesia and Nepal—and so too did child soldier use there. Although this is fewer than the preceding four years, the Coalition's research reveals a number of disturbing findings that make it clear that the efforts to date have been insufficient.

The first of these findings is perhaps the most stark. It is this: when armed conflict breaks out, reignites or intensifies, children will almost inevitably become involved as soldiers. The Central African Republic, Chad, Iraq, Somalia and Sudan (Darfur) are all cases in point.

Next, efforts to demobilize children during conflict have met with only limited success. Peace remains the main hope for securing the release of child soldiers from armed forces and groups, a fact that further reinforces the importance of child protection being integral to peace negotiations, as well as the need for explicit provisions relating to child soldiers in ceasefire and peace agreements.

When armed conflict breaks out, reignites or intensifies, children will almost inevitably become involved as soldiers.

The impact of efforts to end child soldier recruitment and use by armed groups has been similarly limited. Armed groups in at least 24 countries located in every region of the world were known to have recruited under-18s and many have used them in hostilities. Many have proved resistant to pressure and persuasion. Their widely diverse characters, aims and methods, and the varied environments in which they operate militate against generic solutions. Effective strategies must be multifaceted and context-specific. Above all, they must address root causes. Poor governance and its effects, including impoverishment, inequality, discrimination and human rights abuses, are all known to contribute to the risk that children will be recruited by armed groups. While such conditions persist, children will remain vulnerable to involvement in armed forces and groups.

Government and Private Armies Still Use Child Soldiers

The number of governments that deployed children in combat or other frontline duties in their armed forces has not significantly decreased since 2004. Children have been used in armed conflict by government forces in nine situations compared with 10 in the previous four-year period. The most notable offender remains Myanmar, whose armed forces, engaged in long-running counter-insurgency operations against a range of ethnic armed groups, are believed to contain thousands of children. Children were also reported to have been used in hostilities in Chad, the DRC, Somalia, Sudan and Uganda. Additionally, Palestinian children were used on several occasions by defence forces in Israel as human shields. There were reports of child soldier use by Yemeni armed forces in fighting in 2007. A few under-18s in the UK armed forces were sent to Iraq.

The flouting of international standards by governments extends beyond official armed forces. Children in at least 14 countries have been recruited into auxiliary forces linked to national armies; into local-level civilian defence groups established to support counter-insurgency operations; or into militias and armed groups acting as proxies for government forces. In at least eight countries children were used as spies and for other intelligence-gathering purposes, placing them at risk of reprisals and ignoring government responsibilities to provide protection and reintegration assistance.

Lessons Not Learned

Despite growing knowledge of best practices for the disarmament, demobilization and reintegration (DDR) of child soldiers, lessons learned from past efforts have continued to be overlooked in the implementation of official programs. In many DDR processes the needs of child soldiers were not prioritized and in some were entirely overlooked. Reintegration programs were frequently not tailored to their specific needs and have suffered from chronic under-funding.

The repetition of mistakes has been acute in relation to girls. The special needs and vulnerabilities of girls affected by armed conflict have long been recognized, yet they are not well served by DDR processes. The vast majority of girls associated with fighting forces do not participate in official DDR programs and are not catered for in post-demobilization support. Specialized medical care for physical injury resulting from rape or sexually transmitted diseases is rarely available. Girl mothers and their children, often born of rape, are known to be particularly vulnerable, but continue to suffer stigmatization and rejection by their families and communities.

Universal responsibilities under the Optional Protocol to protect children against recruitment and to promote the recovery and reintegration of former child soldiers have yet to be fully realized. When former child soldiers flee their country of origin, asylum processes and special measures facilitating their recognition as refugees are frequently lacking in destination countries, as is the provision of adequate services for their recovery and social reintegration. The legal framework to criminalize the recruitment and use of child soldiers and to establish extraterritorial jurisdiction over such crimes is also far from complete.

Placing children's rights ahead of military needs requires far-reaching shifts in values and attitudes.

Children's Rights Must Come First

Finally, many state parties have undermined the spirit, if not the letter, of the Optional Protocol by continuing to target under-18s for military recruitment. While a number of states have raised the age of voluntary military recruitment within the past four years, at least 63 countries permitted the voluntary recruitment of children by their armed forces; 26 were known to have under-18s in the ranks. Others introduced children, often at a very young age, to military culture through military training in schools, cadet corps and various other youth initiatives.

Placing children's rights ahead of military needs requires far-reaching shifts in values and attitudes. Until it is accepted that childhood extends to 18, and that the spirit of the Protocol expects more of states than just amending the age of conscription, children will continue to be at risk of becoming soldiers, especially in times of crisis.

Bolivia's Children Labor in Dangerous Coal Mines

Laura Baas

According to researcher Laura Baas, in the mines in the south central region of Bolivia, children in large numbers work either in support of the miners or directly in the mines themselves. Especially dangerous is the work inside the mines, where deaths and crippling injuries are common and child workers often replace older miners who have been fatally injured. Baas argues that more attention needs to be paid to these young workers, especially to adolescents, who are often ignored as most child labor eradication projects have been focused on younger children. Laura Baas is a researcher and writer for the IREWOC (International Research on Working Children) Worst Forms of Child Labour in Latin America Project, focusing on research in Bolivia. She has also conducted research in Nicaragua and El Salvador.

As you read, consider the following questions:

1. In Potosí, Bolivia, what are some common activities that young people do in the mining industry?

2. What do teachers say about the school performance of children who work in the mining industry?

3. What recommendations does Baas suggest to eradicate child labor in the Bolivian mines?

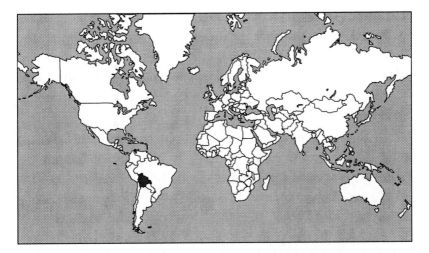

The IREWOC [Foundation for International Research on Working Children] research on the worst forms of child labour in the mining sector of Bolivia took place in two towns of the department of Potosí, Llallagua and the city of Potosí [in Southern Central Bolivia], where tin and silver mining occurs. The mining town of Potosí has around 160,000 inhabitants while Llallagua has 45,000 inhabitants. Although in colonial times the city of Potosí was densely populated and contributed for a large part to the income of the Spanish Crown through the exploitation of the silver and tin holding Cerro Rico, nowadays the whole department of Potosí is the most deprived in Bolivia. The department of Potosí has a population of 709,013 inhabitants (census 2001), of whom 70% are poor.

Mining Statistics in Bolivia

Estimates of child employment in the mining sector vary from 120,000 children in the whole of Bolivia to several hundreds in specific towns. One estimate puts the children working in the mines of Potosí at 147 boys and 28 girls. Differences are usually due to different research methods and varying definitions of child labour. The present research, however, estimates that some 700 adolescents are working inside the mining shafts in Potosí. This number excludes the children living at the Cerro Rico who help their parents to sort through debris and who account for several hundreds more. Fewer children and adolescents, but still a few hundred, are involved in mining in Llallagua.

In Bolivia, mining is considered one of the worst forms of child labour by the government. The Ministry of Labour established a special committee, *Comisión de Erradicación Progresiva del Trabajo Infantil* [Commission for Progressive Eradication of Child Labor] (CEPTI), to work on the eradication of child labour. In the period 2002–6, CEPTI implemented a specific project for the Eradication of Child Labour in Mining (PETIM). The project was subcontracted to CARE [an international humanitarian agency] in Potosí and to CEPROMIN [a non-governmental mining organization] in Llallagua and was financed by the US Department of Labour (USDOL). The results are briefly discussed below in the paragraph on interventions.

The present research . . . estimates that some 700 adolescents are working inside the mining shafts in Potosí.

Mining activities are organised according to a cooperative system. At the Cerro Rico in Potosí there are 37 cooperatives with over 14,000 miners. At the Cerro Rico mountain in Potosí, mining activities are almost entirely limited to extracting ore from within the mine shafts (mainly silver and tin); in the Siglo XX mining district of Llallagua, however, men work inside the mine shafts to extract the ore, whilst all miners (including women) are also involved in the further processing of the ore outside the mines. This process entails crushing the ore with a heavy half-moon shaped rock and then applying various xanthates [an acid salt] in a flotation process to isolate the metals. . . .

Children in Mining

Mining in Potosí and Llallagua can be divided into two phases: extracting the ore from the mines and isolating the metal. Extraction takes place inside the shafts and is performed by men and boys. Isolating the metal from the ore takes place outside the mines, in plants of varying sizes called *ingenios*; this is carried out by both males and females. Children who take part in the process fall into two distinct groups: those younger than 14, and adolescents between 14 and 18. Furthermore, about half of the adolescent miners in Potosí are migrants from the countryside; there are very few migrants in Llallagua.

In Potosí, children who live by the Cerro Rico mountain, where their parents work as guards (*guardas*) at the mine entrance, help out with all sorts of activities that come with their parents' job; the *guardas* make sure that no one but authorised miners enter the mine, they guard the perforating machines, helmets and boots of the miners and sell food and drinks to them. Young boys and girls also work around the mines sweeping up the leftover ore and debris. This work is called *picha*. The work that children do can take between 2 and 6 hours a day, depending on what exactly has to be done. Both boys and girls combine work with school. The work in itself is not particularly heavy or dangerous, but it does put children in a vulnerable and undesirable position. The houses where the *guardas* live with their children have to be manned 24 hours a day; children are sometimes alone at home and frequently have to deal with the miners, who can be drunk or aggressive.

The adolescents in Potosí who enter the mines work 5 to 6 days a week, and between 4 and 10 hours a day, depending on whether they also go to school or not. Some pupils only work during the weekends and school holidays. The adolescents who work inside the shafts perform various jobs:

• Perforating assistants: Perforation entails using various tools to chip away at the underground stone, to find ore. The activity requires a lot of strength and so adolescents limit their participation to assisting the older miners, by passing the tools (drilling machine, hammer, metal pins) and by carrying away the rocks and stones.

• Transporting ore inside and outside the mine: Miners use metal wagons (*carros*) to transport the ore towards the exit and throw it onto a big pile (*desmonte*). Inside the mines they use wheelbarrows to move the ore from one place to another.

• Preparing explosives: Producing sticks of dynamite is part of the daily work of (adolescent) miners. This is obviously a dangerous job.

The adolescents in Potosí who enter the mines work 5 to 6 days a week, and between 4 and 10 hours a day, depending on whether they also go to school or not.

In Llallagua, male adolescents of 14 years and older work underground, where they perform similar jobs to their equals in Potosí. The work in and around the *ingenios* is carried out by children of all ages, and by girls as well as boys. In the *ingenios*, the youngest children participate in all activities, including crushing ore with a *quimbalete* (heavy half-moon stone) and preparing the mixture of water, diesel and xanthate. Adolescents work full time, while children under 14 work a few hours a day or full days in the weekends. Although the work in the *ingenios* is done by both sexes, there are more male adolescents involved with crushing and sieving than are girls, who are usually occupied with selling food and drinks to the workers.

In Potosí, adolescent as well as adult miners claim to be satisfied with their income, which they say is reasonably high because of the metal prices over the last couple of years. They earn between 50 and 100 Bolivianos a day (5–10 euros). This can add up to 1,000–3,000 Bolivianos per month (100–300 euros). In Llallagua, prices for the metals are the same as in Potosí, but there is less metal to be found in the shafts. Miners here complain that they earn little money, or sometimes nothing at all.

Risks and Consequences of Mining

The circumstances in which children work in mining in Potosí and Llallagua are harsh and can be very exhausting. The work inside the mines is especially dangerous; there is always the risk of explosions or cave-ins. Also, many miners suffer from serious pulmonary diseases such as silicosis, popularly called *mal de mina* or miners' disease. Working in the *ingenios* is also risky because of the poisonous xanthates and the heavy instruments used. Living at the Cerro Rico and conducting *picha*, sorting through debris, is detrimental because of the instruments used, the dust it produces, the cold climate and poor living conditions.

NGO [non-governmental organization] employees, teachers and parents also expressed worries about young children being at risk in the presence of drunken miners. Mining culture involves the consumption of [considerable] amounts of alcohol, which creates loyalty within the group. Adolescent miners are especially vulnerable amongst this drunken behaviour.

Where younger children still combine work with school, few adolescents do the same.

Teachers and school directors mentioned that young children who help their parents in *picha* or *ingenio* work are especially tired at school and have problems concentrating. Dropout and repetition, however, is not only due to mining work but even more to a lack of motivation from parents. Parents explained how they let the children themselves decide about enrolment and attendance.

Child Labour in the Coal Mines of Kyrgyzstan

Kylych is one of dozens, possibly hundreds of children working in the abandoned Soviet-era coal mines in the mountains of southern Kyrgyzstan.

He knows what he does is extremely dangerous. He says he has seen his friends die and has been trapped inside himself.

But, he says, he has no choice. The US$3 a day he makes is crucial to his family's survival.

"I'd rather go to school . . . but I need to help the family," he says.

Natalia Antelava, "Child Labour in Kyrgyz Coal Mines,"
BBC News, August 24, 2007.

Where younger children still combine work with school, few adolescents do the same. Some, however, do manage to study at high school or university in the evenings while working in the mines during the day, although this is an exhausting combination. Most of the adolescents working in the mine shafts don't consider it an option to leave mining and to start studying or find another type of job, partly because of a lack of alternatives and partly because mining is a difficult sector to leave once one is integrated. The last comment is based on the high level of loyalty that is created among co-workers and towards bosses in the mining sector.

Why Children Work in Mining

Mining has been taking place in Potosí and Llallagua for hundreds of years. Other productive sectors have barely been developed. *Guarda* families are poor and live with very few other work opportunities, so their children help by contributing to the household income. In the *ingenios* in Llallagua, the same family system can be found; children help their parents with their daily work and are allotted specific tasks, including sieving and crushing ore, and cooking and selling food.

Many serious accidents happen in mining; miners often die young, or are severely injured, preventing them from working. In cases of death or serious injury, and in the absence of an insurance system, children often take over income generating activities. Many children also work because presently metals fetch high prices. Especially in Potosí, young boys currently try to work as much as possible in the mines. Migrants, who come from the deprived high plains of Potosí and Oruro, bring their younger brothers or sons to the city of Potosí, to earn even more during periods of high prices.

People in the Bolivian *altiplano* region are of Quechua and Aymara origin. In these families it is common for children to actively take part in income generating activities and to perform household work. From an early age onwards they are responsible for their own chores as part of their socialisation. Children are considered fit enough to be a miner around the age of 14 and from then on participate in all aspects of mining culture.

Many serious accidents happen in mining: miners often die young, or are severely injured, preventing them from working.

In general, these young miners continue to be employed in mining due to a failing implementation of anti-child labour laws as well as an employer preference to hire youths (they consider them easier to control than their older colleagues). Mining corporations continue to employ under aged miners because they are not prevented from doing so by inspecting (governmental) institutions.

Interventions

From 2002–2006 the USDOL financed the PETIM [Eradication of Child Labour in Mining] project. . . . The major focus of PETIM was on improving education in the mining districts by collaborating with 33 (mostly primary) education centres in Potosí and Llallagua. School teachers and directors were enthusiastic about the project because of the positive outcomes such as improvement of the construction of school buildings, new chairs and tables, and information materials about child labour and mining for awareness raising activities with teachers and pupils. The project wanted to show that not only poverty and lack of productive opportunities forced children into labour, but that mining norms and traditions tend to accept child labour. CARE and USDOL report that through the *PETIM* project, 10% of the 602 participating children got out of mining and the other 90% reduced its number of working hours.

MOLDNATs in Llallagua runs a project that focuses on adolescent miners. MOLDNATs is a group of child labourers that strives for the eradication of child labour in mining, and searches for alternative employment. It is a project that works through peer pressure. Adolescents who used to work in mining try to make other adolescent miners aware of the risks of working inside the shafts. According to members of the group, many of the *mineritos* have left mining and have started to work in other sectors. The group focuses on the importance of education.

Projects to eradicate child labour from mining have mostly focused on meeting the basic needs of people living in mining areas. Unfortunately, political [lobbying] from NGOs and collaboration between mining federations and cooperatives and the local government labour offices has been lacking.

Recommendations

Some recommendations for the eradication of child labour from mining are:

• NGOs should direct more attention towards projects for adolescents. Most projects have been focused on younger children (until 12) and less attention has been paid to the prospects of the older ones. Stimulating technical education for adolescents could be a solution to the lack of opportunities. NGOs should pressure the government to offer higher education on a more structural basis, so that youths can become professionals and not be included in the mining sector.

• NGOs should pressure the government into allotting more funds and personnel to the formalisation of mining, especially in Potosí where anti-child labour regulations are not being upheld. In Llallagua, the mining federation's structural system of age control (anyone under 18 is denied access) has resulted in less child labour in the Llallagua mines. (During the fieldwork no one under 18 was spotted inside the mines, but outside in the *ingenios*, however, there were many children and adolescents working.) NGOs and GOs [government organizations] should work together with mining federations and cooperatives when implementing anti-child labour laws, so as not to let the federations and cooperatives feel excluded from their own sector. Formalisation of the mining sector should focus on the implementation of anti-child labour laws, through strict age inspections, while simultaneously improving the general labour conditions. Better labour conditions, such as mechanization (better supply of air and electricity, decreased risk of cave-ins), will lead to fewer fatal accidents and thus reduce the need for children and adolescents to start working in an attempt to replace the older generation.

• NGOs should lobby for the professionalisation of *guarda* work. Their goal should be to remove the homes of the *guarda* away from the mine's vicinity, thus moving their children away from the direct risks and dangers presented by the mines and the miners, and from their contact with mining that may lead to their eventual employment in the sector.

• NGOs and GOs could improve (or lobby for improvement of) the infrastructure and resources of schools that haven't been upgraded yet by the PETIM project. Schools should also integrate the theme of (the dangers of) mining into their curriculum in order to continuously make children aware of the dangers of the sector.

England's Working Children Need More Protection

P.J. White

According to P.J. White, even everyday jobs can be hazardous to young people if they work too many hours or if they are not supervised properly. For this reason, England's laws that allow children to be treated as unimportant, part-time workers need to be overhauled to prevent severe injuries and even deaths. White asserts that children need to be protected at least as much as adult, full-time workers, yet this is not the case. Instead, he states, they are accorded fewer protections. P.J. White writes for New Statesman *magazine.*

As you read, consider the following questions:

1. According to P.J. White, what are some of the ways that children are injured on the job?

2. What types of jobs do young people do besides babysitting and delivering newspapers?

3. Why is existing legislation not enough in White's opinion, and what should the government do to help working children?

Child protection is more fashionable in some places than others. It wasn't much in evidence at the butcher's shop where 14-year-old Sam Crosby lost all the fingers of his right

P.J. White, "Where Children Come Cheap: Our Wrap-'em-in-Cotton-Wool Approach to the Young Stops at the Workplace," *New Statesman*, vol. 132, January 12, 2004, pp. 36–38. Copyright © 2004 *New Statesman*, Ltd. Reproduced by permission.

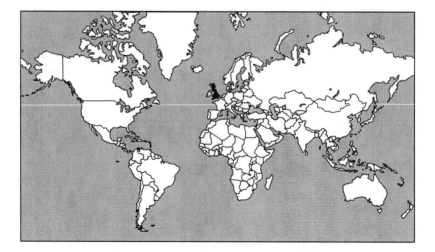

hand while making sausages. Or on the stall in a Hull [Kingston upon Hull, a city in Yorkshire, England] pub car park where Peter Parish, also aged 14, tried to refuel a still-running, petrol-fuelled generator.

Sam was working as a Saturday lad in a shop in Littleworth, Staffordshire. His employer was fined 8,000 [pounds sterling] in October [2003] for various health and safety offences. They included removing the restrictor plate to the mincing machine, which isn't a brilliant piece of child protection, whichever way you look at it. Nor was the district judge in Hull minded to use the law to protect others. When Peter's employer admitted leaving him unsupervised and untrained to work a doughnut stall, he received a conditional discharge. Peter underwent six weeks of skin grafts.

Child Labor Safety Rules Are Ignored

There is something curious about this relaxed attitude to damaging children at work. It jars with what we expect of our highly regulated, wrap-'em-in-cotton-wool approach to children. It also conflicts with general expectations of our workplaces, where, by popular reputation, no one can move without tripping over a health and safety regulation.

Local education authorities have a legal responsibility to register and monitor child employment, issuing permits to anyone wanting to employ 13- to 16-year-olds of compulsory school-going age. But their approach is seriously laid back. Most authorities ask employers to carry out a risk assessment prior to issuing a permit. Do they then ask to see the assessment? Not generally, according to the Health and Safety Executive. It finds that authorities "very rarely check that a risk assessment is being adhered to".

There is something curious about this relaxed attitude to damaging children at work.

In a survey, 66 per cent said they "have never followed up a risk assessment"; 31 per cent said they would follow up if an issue arose. The permit system itself is widely ignored, yet few local authorities have child employment officers actively investigating breaches. Some authorities have a policy of not prosecuting.

The government has recognised the problem. It set up a working group on child employment at the Better Regulation Task Force in October [2003], to report this month [January 2004]. The leader of the study group, Simon Petch, accepts that, "there are too many examples where the law has not achieved its aims and children have been found to be working excessive hours, or in prohibited premises such as commercial kitchens".

Work Is a Normal Adolescent Experience

Not all child work is exploitative. Few people think that work is essentially a bad thing for children. Young people, employers and parents generally welcome it. It promotes independence, self-esteem and skill acquisition. It keeps potentially idle hands busy. The question is whether children's work is properly regulated—at present, it is in practice less regulated than adult work.

Work is a normal adolescent experience. Most children have had at least one job by the time they leave school. There are no official figures, says Jim McKechnie of Paisley University, who has studied the subject extensively. But snapshots give a consistent picture of there being between 1.1 million and 1.7 million under-16s in some kind of paid employment. "If you ask how many have ever worked by the time they reach 16, then the extrapolated figure goes to between 2.2 and 2.6 million."

Children's work is no longer confined to babysitting and newspaper delivery.

Teachers say work often affects children's school performance. "There is research evidence of a connection between excessive working and poorer commitment to school," says McKechnie. Excessive working is defined as ten hours or more. What is not clear is whether disaffected children opt out from school and get part-time jobs or whether the commitment to a part-time job drags down schoolwork. Probably a bit of both.

Children's work is no longer confined to babysitting and newspaper delivery. Many under-16s are quietly getting on with what anyone would recognise as proper adult jobs. Margaret Berry, senior environmental health officer with Calderdale Council, surveyed pupils at two local schools. She found that 44 per cent were working. Most were employed in catering, preparing and serving food, and serving in shops. Nearly a quarter of boys in one school were doing labouring, fencing or joinery work.

Children Will Work at Almost Any Jobs

A similar picture emerges around the country. Workers for Connexions, the youth advisory service, report kids doing almost anything. They work in hotels, cafes and bars. They

"Fast Food Sweatshops" in Great Britain

One successful example of effective labour inspection is the investigation of a McDonalds' franchise in Camberley, Great Britain, where what is believed to be the biggest ever fine for a child labour offence was levied on a McDonalds' franchise holder.

The £12,400 (US$20,000) penalty followed an investigation in which school-age children were found to be working up to sixteen hours a day at the local McDonalds restaurant in what was described on the news as a "fast-food sweatshop".

International Labour Office, Child Labour: A Textbook for University Students, *2004.*

work in family businesses, on farms and for scrap metal firms, on markets, in supermarkets and doing all kinds of shop work. Seventy-five per cent of them work illegally; roughly 10 per cent say they have truanted in order to work.

Pay rates for children can range from 1 [pounds sterling] or 2 [pounds sterling] an hour to close to the minimum wage (which naturally excludes them, as it does 16-and 17-year-olds). Some children are undoubtedly working to ease the pressure on family budgets. But there is no simplistic relationship between school-age workers and poverty, McKechnie says when he first started going into schools, "we were told that all we would be studying was social class." The stereotype was that children from poorer families were likely to work. But some studies suggest the opposite. "Children from areas of extreme poverty have fewer job opportunities and no local labour market networks to tap into."

Child Labor and the Law

Prosperous Surrey is indeed where most of the infringements of child labour laws have been prosecuted. Here, there is a high demand for low-paid casual workers; and the county council has hired the country's most prolific prosecutor of illegal child employers, the former police officer Ian Hart. His most recent prosecution, in October [2003], was of Sainsbury's for breaches of permit requirements and permitted hours legislation at one of its branches in Leatherhead. Hart, whose personal tally of prosecutions exceeds 20, has gained court victories over big names including McDonald's, Tesco, Forbuoys news agents and Woolworths. He remains shocked at the cavalier attitude of major employers. Of one supermarket, he says: "I could not believe that, despite all our efforts in attempting to work with the company and following up with written warnings, they had the audacity to carry on blatantly ignoring the law."

There are three main strands to the legal controls. Stone occupations and industries are deemed too dangerous altogether and children are banned from employment in such areas as factory work, selling petrol and working in slaughterhouses. Equally, age-related maximum hours are set for weekdays and weekends, so that children do not work too many hours, or too early or too late during the school term. Finally, there is the permit system.

Children are allowed to do light work. But what an adult regards as light work may not be experienced as such by a 13-year-old.

"The vast majority [of children] don't work in factories and don't work in extreme types of employment," says McKechnie. "But because they are doing delivery work or shop work doesn't mean that they are not at risk." In fact, studies show that most accidents to children occur while they are making deliveries. Fourteen-year-old Ryan Pettigrew was killed while delivering newspapers in June 2001. His round included a road with a 60 mph speed limit which in parts had no pavements, and he had neither helmet nor reflective clothing.

Children are allowed to do light work. But what an adult regards as light work may not be experienced as such by a 13-year-old. Consider that the 13-year-old is already committed to 28 hours per week at school, has homework and has perhaps walked or run to get to the workplace. A good and willing worker, especially one as cheap as a schoolchild, will be offered more work, especially at busy times.

At the very least, children at work should have the same level of protection that adults have.

A Complete Overhaul of Child Labor Laws Is Needed

The European Working Time Directive holds no sway when it comes to children in the workplace: in the run-up to Christmas, for instance, Sam Crosby, who was injured at the butcher's shop, had been working extremely long hours. His fatigue no doubt contributed to his injury. The Health and Safety Executive knows of 31 reportable accidents involving under-16s at work over the past two years, including 16 major injuries and one fatality. But accidents will be under-reported, especially those to children employed in illegal industries.

At the very least, children at work should have the same level of protection that adults have. To achieve this, the government's new task force group, which aims simply to improve the implementation of existing child labour legislation, is not enough. What is needed, instead, is a complete overhaul of a law that allows children to be treated as a casual, part-time and dispensable workforce.

South Asian Bonded Child Laborers Suffer a Wide Range of Abuses

The Child Workers in Asia Foundation

In investigating the practice of bonded child labor—a form of slavery—in Asia, the Child Workers in Asia Foundation discovered that children are subjected to horrific work conditions and treated virtually as slaves. Bonded children are usually given over to employers to pay a family debt, but their pay is so low that they may never escape an endless cycle of paying off their employers. The authors assert that uneducated, unschooled child workers are treated in an inhumane fashion, and as a result, they withdraw completely and are often unable to advocate for themselves or even to understand their situation. The Child Workers in Asia Foundation (CWA), established in 1985, provides support for child workers in Asia and for the nongovernmental organizations working with them.

As you read, consider the following questions:

1. According to the article, from what social stratum of society are child bonded workers usually taken?

2. In what three ways can children enter into bondage?

3. How are bonded child laborers usually treated by society, including the police and judiciary officials?

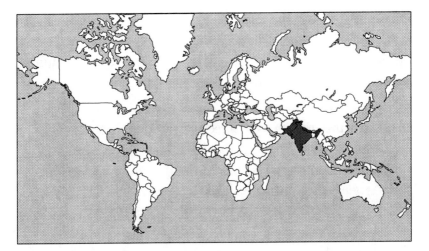

Bondage is a form of slavery. When adults, children or families are bonded, they are denied their freedom to change employment and often their freedom of movement. They are forced to work for little or no wages, undermining their freedom as economic agents. They are denied full freedom to pursue their lives and their own development with dignity.

Bondage and Obligations

Bondage is generally understood to be a form of forced labour, but is often not entirely involuntary. In many cases, those who are bonded work for their employer under some form of promise, contract, or agreement to which they have consented. For some, consent is a matter of custom and history in the communities in which they live. This consent is understood to entail an obligation of the workers to labour under whatever conditions the employer chooses to impose.

In cases of enforcement of bondage the labourer is often subjected to verbal and physical threats against themselves and their family, withholding of payment for work already completed, physical abuse including beatings and torture, forced dispossession, confiscation of belongings, and other gross abuses to prevent the exercise of their human rights and labour rights. In many cases, these contracts and agreements, and the abusive methods used to enforce them, are upheld and enforced by local laws, courts and communities.

When the dignity and integrity of the person, be they child or adult, is so obviously violated, it is clear that their consent cannot be used to bind them to work which is exploitative and which violates their rights.

However, though a contract or agreement may exist between a labourer and an employer, this should not mean that the labourer cannot choose to end their employment when they wish even if included in the contract. No employer has the right to force any labourer to continue to work when they are unwilling to do so.

When the dignity and integrity of the person, be they child or adult, is so obviously violated, it is clear that their consent cannot be used to bind them to work which is exploitative and which violates their rights. It is not consistent with principles of justice and human rights that an individual can enter into an agreement such that they no longer have any power over themselves.

Customary or historical obligations take the form of status or hierarchical obligations within a society or community, where marginalised and socially excluded persons, families, family members, and communities are bound to their employers on the basis of their lower or marginal status. These obligations are embedded in a more general environment where status is widely accepted as sufficient grounds for systematic discrimination, enslavement, and general denial of rights and equal treatment. These status obligations can also be felt to be a duty owed by those bonded or as an inevitable and essential feature of their lives.

The violations against bonded labourers in these cases are a result of specific sanctions and prohibitions from their employers, and are reinforced by more general social sanctions against them which often manifest in physical violence and terror, and are sometimes enforced through legal or administrative systems. Whatever their interpretation, these duties and obligations and their enforcement are generally compelling as a matter of social life.

Bondage in South Asia is generally characterisable in these terms. The bonded labour system in South Asia is among the oldest forms of forced labour and accounts for the greatest number of forced labourers in the contemporary world. As we might expect, the incidence of bonded labour has been and continues to be severely high among members of the lowest social groups in the hierarchically organised caste system in India; among indigenous minorities and lower castes in Nepal and religious minorities in Pakistan. Persons born in these communities have traditionally been bonded to higher caste employers for generations. Entire families, including children, are usually bonded to one particular family of high social status and all members of the family, including children, labour for the employers.

Children in bondage suffer from cumulative effects throughout their lives of the widespread denial of education, intellectual development and recognition of their inherent dignity as persons.

Bondage and Social Exclusion

Whatever the justifications or causes, systems of bondage are systems for violations of rights and denial of entitlements. Whether or not an agreement or customary social obligation is a central element of the bondage, bondage excludes persons from equal treatment and equal access to the benefits of society. Children in bondage suffer from cumulative effects throughout their lives of the widespread denial of education, intellectual development and recognition of their inherent dignity as persons.

Bondage and Debt

The specific manifestations of bonded labour in which a person is compelled to work for someone from whom he or she has received an advance is termed 'debt bondage'. In this manifestation, an advance is used as an instrument of coercion to force persons, and often their families and descendants, to work for an employer. While borrowing money from an employer is not unusual, in bonded labour cases the 'debt' is enforced through exploitation and denial of rights.

As labour relations become increasingly informed by economic and financial forces, the use of advances to reinforce and justify situations of bondage and to exploit social discrimination in new ways has increased. Many persons who might not be bonded directly through status obligations come to be bonded through economic and financial obligations, which can then form the basis for new systems of systematic discrimination as these advances are transformed by employers into debt which is to be held by the family and sometimes also descendants.

As a result of their poverty, their lack of freedom in movement, and the stigma and prejudice they encounter as lower caste families, bonded labourers are typically compelled to seek cash or goods from their employers specifically, who treat these advances as legitimately enforceable through further demands for labour. The labourers are compelled to work to 'repay' this debt within the context of their existing condition of bondage under that employer. Conditions of work are made so that their 'debt' is increased through the application of extortionate rates of interest; higher than normal charges by employers for food, accommodation, transportation, or tools; and wages which are not high enough to allow the worker to repay the advance except through additional work. In many cases, the 'debt' is actually a payment made to the worker instead of regular wages and is one aspect of a more comprehensive exploitation of the worker and their relations. The employer creates a liability which they then manipulate to exploit the worker and guarantee access to and power of disposal over the fruits of his labour.

Debt as an instrument of coercion is also common in cases of trafficking, where an individual is forced to pay their trafficker for the expense of being trafficked. In such cases, the 'debt' is not an advance, but a false claim that the person trafficked owes something to their trafficker. In cases like this, the debt is part of a chain of coercion and exploitation.

In all of these situations, the debts themselves are illegitimate as their terms and conditions are usually either unspecified or are not followed, and the agreement is generally highly exploitative, coercive, or endangers the debtor. The fact of bondage alone makes illegitimate any claim of debt.

Bondage and Children

In the case of children working as part of a bonded family or working to repay an inherited debt, bonded child labour can only be properly understood in the context of the bonded labour system as a whole. Bonded child labour cannot be addressed without addressing the bonded labour of adults and families.

Children enter into bondage in three main ways: they can work as part of a bonded family, they can inherit a debt from a parent or other family member, or they can be pledged individually to work in various sectors including beedi-rolling [cigarette], silk reeling and domestic work, to name just a few. As with adult bonded labourers, the majority of bonded child labourers are found in the informal sector.

In family bondage situations the labour of the whole family is required to meet an obligation of an authoritative mem-

Children at the Silk Looms

Sitting at crowded silk looms for long stretches of time exposes children to a variety of health problems. The rooms are often damp and poorly ventilated; children sit with their legs tucked under them or dangling down into the pit underneath the loom. The crowded work environment encourages the spread of contagious diseases, especially tuberculosis and digestive disorders. Poor lighting and constant visual strain damages the eyesight. The fine silk threads cut the fingers, and the cuts are difficult to heal properly.

Human Rights Watch, Small Change:
Bonded Child Labor in India's Silk Industry, *2003*

ber of the family or as a matter of the family's status. Obligations in such cases may be debt contracted by the family head or an inherited debt or other intergenerational, status-based obligation. It can also follow that the family stays together, where all family members fall into the situation of bondage as their contribution to the family finances. A family may be so obligated to their employer that they are unable to refuse demands from employers to take a child for whatever purpose. In the event of the obligation being unfulfilled within the lifetime of the parents, a child may inherit these obligations and continue to work to fulfil them, sometimes being forced to pass them on to their own children and future generations.

Children bonded as part of a family and children who inherit bonded debts are often working in systems of agricultural bonded labour, or else are assisting their families in places such as brick kilns or stone quarries. Children also commonly help with home-based production work (only some of which is bonded labour), although employers who contract out such work are taking increasing care not to have direct dealings with the children involved, so as to minimise the risk of being caught violating labour laws.

In the event of the obligation being unfulfilled within the lifetime of the parents, a child may inherit these obligations and continue to work to fulfil them.

The individual pledging of children is a comparatively newer but growing phenomenon wherein middlemen (or less frequently, employers) recruit children by giving the children's parents an advance. Sometimes the pressure to accept the advance is severe. Sometimes these pledged children are then trafficked from rural areas to urban areas to work. Employers generally seek to keep the bonded child labourers out of sight, for instance by having them work in small production units rather than in factories.

Payment arrangements differ; some pledged children are kept in bondage as mere collateral and interest for a loan, which must later be paid back in one lump sum (as in the beedi industry). Others are allowed to gradually repay their loans, but their wages (which are typically paid by piece-rates) are almost always too low to allow the loans to be repaid in a reasonable amount of time. In fact, the debts often increase due to high interest rates, charges for living expenses and wage-deductions for mistakes.

Causes of Bonded Child Labour

Social exclusion is a central cause, and poverty a common feature, of bonded labour and other types of forced labour.

Worldwide, indigenous and tribal peoples and socially excluded communities such as those from lower castes, religious minorities, and the uneducated and illiterate commonly remain subject to forced labour and other forms of labour exploitation, discrimination in access to training and employment, and other ills that accompany their marginal status. Women and children bonded labourers face additional exploitation based on gender and age discrimination. The vulnerability to exploitation implied by being so excluded may determine whether indebtedness becomes bondage. Active discrimination against the socially excluded often means they are expected to render service and surrender their rights as a matter of course.

Poverty is often a feature of bonded labour since bonded labourers are typically landless, without assets, underpaid and overworked. The lack of social entitlement and livelihood creates a state of slavery. Poverty can also be seen as a consequence of bondage insofar as the bondage may exacerbate and entrench the factors that lead to both further bondage and poverty.

Aggravating factors include the existence of feudal or other hierarchically structured agricultural systems or communities, lack of political will for effective social change, prevalence of education systems that perpetuate social inequalities and general injustice, anti-people development paradigms, trends toward the informalisation of labour [work in small sweatshops, homes and informal venues], inadequate legislative frameworks, ineffective enforcement of policies, desire for and liberal use of cheap labour in production processes, and inadequate living wages.

Impacts of Bonded Child Labour

Children in bondage suffer a range of abuses and violations of their rights and dignity. However, the impact of bondage on child labourers is not unique to bondage, as many child workers suffer the same exploitation that bonded child labourers do. That being said, the level of exploitation associated with bondage and slavery is manifested in the extreme degrees to which children are made to endure long hours, dangerous and unhealthy work and working conditions, violence and abuse, humiliation, discrimination, and a general lack of access to other rights such as to education, participation in culture and recreation.

Children in bondage tend to be engaged in brutally exploitative and harmful physical labour in fields, factories and homes. They are required to work long hours with intense workloads. As a result they experience fatigue, muscular and skeletal problems, deterioration of their eyesight, and other problems that negatively impact their health and development. In addition to these direct impacts of their work, they are also often made to work under conditions which contribute to the spread of disease, and which amplify the negative impact of the work they do on their bodies.

Children are often beaten or tortured, such as being burnt with metal rods, for working too slowly or for offering any resistance whatsoever to the demands of their employer.

Children forced to sit in small spaces, hunched over, in the same position for long periods of time often suffer from chronic back pain and may develop growth deformities. Children working on looms or processing silk often cut their fingers and hands, and these wounds are often not treated, or are treated in unhygienic and painful ways, such as cauterising the cuts with sulphur. Children are often beaten or tortured, such as being burnt with metal rods, for working too slowly or for offering any resistance whatsoever to the demands of their employer.

Children involved in beedi-rolling (a kind of cigarette) suffer from high rates of tuberculosis and other lung diseases. Children working with looms often develop lung and skin diseases caused by prolonged proximity to wool. Children working in agriculture, domestic work, and silver polishing endure constant and unsafe exposure to harmful chemicals. Children working in mines may be exposed to poisonous gases. Children working with gems or other work that requires close examination may experience eye disorders that are normal for 40–50 year olds as early as their 20s.

Complete Subjugation of Bonded Children

For many children, being bonded is part of a more general pattern in their lives of social exclusion and discrimination, and serves to reinforce it. Bonded children are understood by their employers to be at the disposal of the employer, and have very little control over their own lives. As a result, they are often made to submit to unreasonable or humiliating demands and are looked down on by both employers and others. Bonded children may be subject to regular physical and sexual abuse, including torture, either as a form of discipline or as a privilege claimed by the employer. Demands and requests for fair treatment by children and adults who are bonded are often received with scorn, and sometimes worse, by not only their employers, but also by members of society, sometimes including the police and judiciary officials who are responsible for protecting them. In some cases, especially for domestic workers, they are prohibited from interacting socially outside the workplace. Bonded children are often witness to the abuse or humiliation of other children, or of their own and other children's families. When children attempt to escape from their bondage, they are often hunted down. When recovered they are beaten, tortured, and sometimes even killed as a lesson to themselves and others.

As a result, bonded children tend to internalise, distrust and fear others, and lack hope for their future. Sometimes, bonded children are even unable to imagine or articulate a different situation or treatment for themselves or others.

Whether working with their families or in an individual capacity, bonded children are unlikely to attend school. This is a violation of their rights both to education and to participate in society. Without education, children cannot broadly understand their own situation and the nature of their own and other societies and cultures. This prevents them from engaging with themselves and with others for the purposes of cooperation and development. Universal education is needed for a society to realise the principles of equality and mutual respect, and to ensure that each individual can fully participate in the decisions that shape their lives. Bonded children do not have this opportunity, and the discrimination that it reveals and perpetuates is a lasting barrier to their full development.

Periodical Bibliography

Stephan Bose-O'Reilly,
Beate Lettmeier,
Raffaella Matteucci
Gothe, Christian
Beinhoff, Uwe Siebert,
and Gustav Drasch
"Mercury as a Aerious Health Hazard for Children in Gold Mining Areas," *Environmental Research*, May 2008.

Josh Cable
"Survey Highlights Dangers in Teen Jobs," *Occupational Hazards*, vol. 69, April 2007.

Joanna C. Castro
"The Games Children Play," *Irawaddy*, December 2003, pp. 20–21.

Richel Dursin
"Indonesia: Virtual Slave Labor Awaits Child Domestic Workers," Inter Press Service, April 12, 2006.

Kurt Henne and
David Moseley
"Combating the Worst Forms of Child Labor in Bolivia," *Human Rights*, Winter 2005.

Mark P. Lagon
"Human Trafficking in China," *DISAM Journal*, March 2008.

Susan McClelland
"Francis Bok, Escaped Slave," *Peace Magazine*, April/June 2004, pp. 16–17.

P.W. Singer
"Children at War," *Military History*, vol. 24, no. 6, September 2007, pp. 50–55.

Camelia M. Tepelus
"Social Responsibility and Innovation on Trafficking and Child Sex Tourism: Morphing of Practice into Sustainable Tourism Policies?" *Tourism & Hospitality Research*, April 2008.

Trafficking in Persons
"Policy Approaches to Trafficking in Persons," Annual 2007.

Janice Windau and
Samuel Meyer
"Occupational Injuries Among Young Workers," *Monthly Labor Review*, October 2005.

CHAPTER 3

Defending Child Labor

For Uzbekistan's Poverty-Stricken Families, Child Labor Is a Necessary Evil

Sunny Ntayombya

In the following viewpoint, Sunny Ntayombya observes that child labor is a more complex issue than many believe. When the British retailer, Tesco, pulled its business from Uzbekistan to protest child labor, it may have had more negative than positive consequences. Shutting down a country's main source of income can cripple the country's economy despite good intentions, worsening the poverty that made child labor necessary in the first place, Ntayombya points out. Instead of idealistic do-gooders telling them what to do, Ntayombya maintains, emerging nations need practical solutions to alleviate the poverty that drives child labor. Sunny Ntayombya lives in Rwanda, where, in addition to writing columns that appear in Rwanda's newspaper The New Times, *he hosts a radio show.*

As you read, consider the following questions:

1. How does Ntayombya feel about exploiting children?

2. What does Ntayombya speculate would happen if western customers boycotted Rwanda's coffee?

3. What solutions does Ntayombya offer besides simply ending child labor?

Sunny Ntayombya, "Child Labour Isn't as Straight Forward as You May Think, " *The New Times* via *Africa News Service*, January 18, 2008. Reproduced by permission.

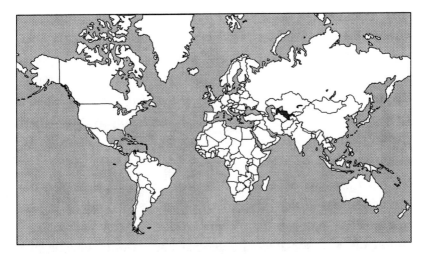

Listening to the BBC's [British Broadcasting Corporation's] flagship news programme, *News Hour*, a few nights ago, I heard a story that got me thinking about one of the largest problems that faces the poorer nations and communities worldwide: child labor.

According to the report, Britain's biggest retailer Tesco on Tuesday [January 2008] said the use of forced child labour in Uzbekistan meant it would no longer buy the country's cotton to make its clothes. In its press statement given the AFP [Agence France-Presse] news agency, Tesco said that, "Following ongoing discussions with campaign groups on the subject of cotton production and the use of child labour . . . we feel the need to re-iterate Tesco's deep concern at the use of child labour . . . the use of organized and forced child labour is completely unacceptable and leads us to conclude that whilst these practices persist in Uzbekistan, we cannot support the use of cotton from Uzbekistan in our clothing."

Child Labor Is a Complex Issue

Personally, I'm totally against the notion of children working under the hot sun, picking cotton for the enrichment of some cotton baron. But it often isn't just a matter of plain exploitation. Let's look at some Uzbek economic figures; Uzbekistan's Gross Domestic Product (GDP) [per capita, meaning the total value of the country's goods and services divided by its population] is only $386 per annum. Let's try to put some perspective to that figure; Rwanda, which is a poor nation, has a GDP [per capita] per annum of $242. That means the average Uzbek makes about Frw [Rwandan Francs] 50,000 more than the average Rwandan on a yearly basis.

Now imagine what would happen if, all of a sudden, western customers of our [Rwandan] coffee decided not to import our number one product. There would be utter bedlam economically and socially. The central bank would hardly have any foreign exchange in its coffers to import essential things like medicines, and the farmers wouldn't have any more money to provide for themselves and their families. Our economy would head in only one direction, down.

Nobody would put children in the fields, neither their parents nor the Uzbek government, unless it was absolutely necessary.

That's what has happened in Uzbekistan due to this well-meaning move. Cotton, like coffee in Rwanda, is this nation's biggest export; in fact, Uzbekistan is the third largest exporter in the world and it is, therefore, probably the mainstay of its economy. This cotton is gathered by hand. What does this mean? It means that, unlike in richer nations where the harvesting is done by machine and therefore capital intensive, the Uzbek cotton industry is labour intensive instead. Can you imagine how many people are employed picking cotton manually? Tens of thousands.

Now, why would children, if the reports are true, be steamrolled into the dusty, hot cotton fields, probably alongside their parents? I put my head to the block and offer this as-

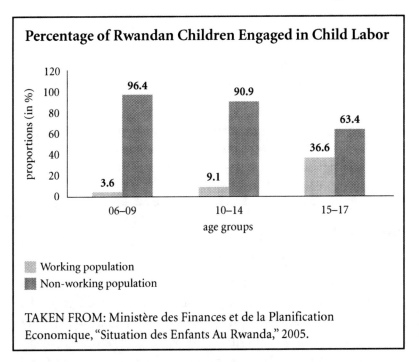

Percentage of Rwandan Children Engaged in Child Labor

TAKEN FROM: Ministère des Finances et de la Planification Economique, "Situation des Enfants Au Rwanda," 2005.

sumption: nobody would put children in the fields, neither their parents nor the Uzbek government, unless it was absolutely necessary.

A Choice of Food or Schooling

Child labour is, as the Tesco's press statement put it, complicated and not one-dimensional as we wish it could be. Let's use some local examples. A rural family often has certain pressures that urbanites, like you and I, and western supermarket chains don't understand. They have very little, and they must survive with whatever means at hand. Very often, the means also include their own children. The children fetch wood, water, work in the gardens and rear the family livestock, if indeed they are lucky enough to have any.

I'm sure that parents know that their children ought to be going to school, but here is the million dollar question: What's more important, food or schooling? Remember that most of

the people that face this stark choice between these two human rights, of food and education, are often the same ones
who can't fulfill both these needs simultaneously. The opportunity cost of feeding and clothing the children is work that
the children shouldn't be doing.

*Instead of agitating against child labour, maybe they
should agitate as strongly for fewer tariffs, less agricultural subsidies and more aid.*

Solving Child Labor Involves Solving Poverty

So, how can we holistically fight child labour without breaking the backs of the parents? First of all, we need to understand that child labour is an issue of poverty and nothing else.
Child labour was prevalent in the West during the 19th and
pre-World War Two 20th century, and came to an end only
when their economies became more mechanized. Therefore, I
believe that third-world nations will bid 'adieu' to this when
they can afford to; when they leave the agrarian base of their
collective economies and mechanize. However, this is a gradual
process that the pressure groups in the West must understand.
Instead of agitating against child labour, maybe they should
agitate as strongly for fewer tariffs, less agricultural subsidies
and more aid.

Child Work Serves a Need in Many Impoverished Nations

Sam Vaknin

In the following viewpoint, Sam Vaknin argues that do-gooders who rail against child labor may be doing more harm than good. In many cases where intervention ended child labor in various countries around the world, children and their families found themselves worse off as a result. Ending child labor without providing a better alternative is not a solution, Vaknin states. Abusive child labor is abhorrent and should be eliminated, he acknowledges, but there are gradations of child work. Some jobs for children are much less heinous than others, and some are even beneficial in developing skills that young people will need later in life. Sam Vaknin is the author of Malignant Self Love–Narcissism Revisited *and* After the Rain—How the West Lost the East. *He is a columnist for* Central Europe Review *and* United Press International (UPI). *He has also served as the economic advisor to the government of Macedonia.*

As you read, consider the following questions:

1. According to Vaknin, how do people of countries such as Thailand, Brazil, or Morocco regard Westerners who campaign against child labor?

2. According to former U.S. labor secretary Robert Reich, what are some unintended negative consequences of stopping child labor?

3. What is a creative solution to the child labor situation that has been proposed by two professors?

From the comfort of their plush offices and five to six figure salaries, self-appointed non-government organizations [NGOs] often denounce child labor as their employees rush from one five star hotel to another, $3,000 subnotebooks and PDAs in hand. The hairsplitting distinction made by the International Labor Organization between "child work" and "child labor" conveniently targets impoverished countries while letting its budget contributors—the developed ones—off the hook.

Reports regarding child labor surface periodically. Children crawling in mines, faces ashen, body deformed. The agile fingers of famished infants weaving soccer balls for their more privileged counterparts in the United States. Tiny figures huddled in sweatshops, toiling in unspeakable conditions. It is all heartrending and it gave rise to a veritable not-so-cottage industry of activists, commentators, legal eagles, scholars, and opportunistically sympathetic politicians.

Child Labor Opponents May Have a Hidden Agenda

Ask the denizens of Thailand, sub-Saharan Africa, Brazil, or Morocco and they will tell you how they regard this altruistic hyperactivity—with suspicion and resentment. Underneath the compelling arguments lurks an agenda of trade protectionism, they wholeheartedly believe. Stringent—and expensive—labor and environmental provisions in international treaties may well be a ploy to fend off imports based on cheap labor and the competition they wreak on well-ensconced domestic industries and their political stooges.

This is especially galling since the sanctimonious West has amassed its wealth on the broken backs of slaves and kids. The 1900 census in the United States found that 18 percent of all children—almost two million in all—were gainfully employed. The Supreme Court ruled unconstitutional laws banning child labor as late as 1916. This decision was overturned only in 1941.

The General Accounting Office published a report last week [September 2002] in which it criticized the Department of Labor for paying insufficient attention to working conditions in manufacturing and mining in the United States where many children are still employed. The Bureau of Labor Statistics pegs the number of working children between the ages of 15–17 in the country at 3.7 million. One in 16 of these worked in factories and construction. More than 600 teens died of work-related accidents in the past 10 years.

The sanctimonious West has amassed its wealth on the broken backs of slaves and kids.

Gradations of Child Labor

Child labor—let alone child prostitution, child soldiers, and child slavery—are phenomena best avoided. But they cannot and should not be tackled in isolation. Nor should underage labor be subjected to blanket castigation. Working in the gold mines or fisheries of the Philippines is hardly comparable to waiting on tables in a Nigerian or, for that matter, American restaurant.

There are gradations and hues of child labor. That children should not be exposed to hazardous conditions, long working hours, used as means of payment, physically punished, or serve as sex slaves is commonly agreed. That they should not help their parents plant and harvest may be more debatable.

As Miriam Wasserman observes in "Eliminating Child Labor", published in the Federal Bank of Boston's Regional Review, second quarter of 2000, it depends on "family income, education policy, production technologies, and cultural norms." About a quarter of children under 14 throughout the world are regular workers. This statistic masks vast disparities between regions such as Africa (42 percent) and Latin America (17 percent).

Working in the gold mines or fisheries of the Philippines is hardly comparable to waiting on tables in a . . . restaurant.

All Children Have a Right to Survive

In many impoverished locales, child labor is all that stands between the family unit and all-pervasive, life threatening, destitution. Child labor declines markedly as income per capita grows. To deprive these bread earners of the opportunity to lift themselves and their families incrementally above malnutrition, disease, and famine—is an apex of immoral hypocrisy.

Quoted by *The Economist*, a representative of the much decried Ecuador Banana Growers Association and Ecuador's Labor Minister, summed up the dilemma neatly: "Just because they are under age doesn't mean we should reject them, they have a right to survive. You can't just say they can't work, you have to provide alternatives."

Regrettably, the debate is so laden with emotions and self-serving arguments that the facts are often overlooked.

The outcry against soccer balls stitched by children in Pakistan led to the relocation of workshops run by Nike and Reebok. Thousands lost their jobs, including countless women and 7,000 of their progeny. The average family income— anyhow meager—fell by 20 percent. Economists Drusilla Brown, Alan Deardorif, and Robert Stern observe wryly:

"While Baden Sports can quite credibly claim that their soccer balls are not sewn by children, the relocation of their production facility undoubtedly did nothing for their former child workers and their families."

Such examples abound. Manufacturers—fearing legal reprisals and "reputation risks" (naming-and-shaming by overzealous NGOs)—engage in preemptive sacking. German garment workshops fired 50,000 children in Bangladesh in 1993 in anticipation of the American never-legislated Child Labor Deterrence Act.

Stopping Child Labor Can Leave Children Worse Off

Quoted by Wasserman, former U.S. labor secretary Robert Reich, notes: "Stopping child labor without doing anything else could leave children worse off. If they are working out of necessity, as most are, stopping them could force them into prostitution or other employment with greater personal dangers.

"The most important thing is that they be in school and receive the education to help them leave poverty."

"*Stopping child labor without doing anything else could leave kids worse off.*"

Contrary to hype, three-quarters of all children work in agriculture and with their families. Less than 1 percent work in mining, and another 2 percent in construction. Most of the rest work in retail outlets and services, including "personal services"—a euphemism for prostitution. UNICEF [United Nations Children's Fund] and the International Labor Organization [ILO] are in the throes of establishing school networks for child laborers and providing their parents with alternative employment.

But this is a drop in the sea of neglect. Poor countries rarely proffer education on a regular basis to more than two thirds of their eligible school-age children. This is especially true in rural areas where child labor is a widespread blight. Education—especially for girls—is considered an unaffordable

161

Westerners Judge Child Labor by False Standards

Equal care must be taken over the fashionable crusade for the elimination of child labour. For, once again, contemporary westerners judge the developing countries by the standards they are lucky enough to enjoy. . . . Approximately 250 million children between the ages of five and fourteen work in developing countries, certainly a far lower proportion of the world's children than ever before in history. Of these, 70 per cent work in agriculture and no more than 10–15 million in export industries, predominantly in south Asia. These children work not because their parents (if they have them) are more wicked than those anywhere else, but because of their poverty. Nothing is better established than the tendency for better-off parents in more prosperous societies to have fewer children and invest more in their education. . . .

The evidence of the impact of rising incomes on child labour is . . . dramatic. Between 1993 and 1998, the income of the poorest 10 per cent of Vietnamese rose by more than a half, in real terms. This led to a sharp reduction in child labour . . . and greater investment in their education. Now suppose that western trade sanctions forced child workers out of export-oriented factories instead. . . . they will do something else: prostitution, for example, or farm labour. . . . Substantial evidence exists that exactly this happened in Bangladesh in the early 1990s, in response to a campaign against Wal-Mart's purchases of clothing made, in part, by children. Thousands were sacked, many of whom moved on to more dangerous and less well-paid jobs.

Martin Wolf, Why Globalization Works, *New Haven, CT: Yale University Press, 2004.*

luxury by many hard-pressed parents. In many cultures, work is still considered to be indispensable in shaping the child's morality and strength of character and in teaching him or her a trade.

The Economist elaborates: "In Africa children are generally treated as mini-adults; from an early age every child will have tasks to perform in the home, such as sweeping or fetching water. It is also common to see children working in shops or on the streets. Poor families will often send a child to a richer relation as a housemaid or houseboy, in the hope that he will get an education."

Abusive child labor is abhorrent and should be banned and eradicated. All other forms should be phased out gradually.

Practical Solutions

A solution recently gaining steam is to provide families in poor countries with access to loans secured by the future earnings of their educated offspring. The idea—first proposed by Jean-Marie Baland of the University of Namur and James A. Robinson of the University of California at Berkeley—has now permeated the mainstream.

Even the World Bank has contributed a few studies, notably, in June [2002], "Child Labor: The Role of Income Variability and Access to Credit Across Countries" authored by Rajeev Dehejia of the NBER [National Bureau of Economic Research] and Roberta Gatti of the Bank's Development Research Group.

Abusive child labor is abhorrent and should be banned and eradicated. All other forms should be phased out gradually. Developing countries already produce millions of unemployable graduates a year—100,000 in Morocco alone. Unemployment is rife and reaches, in certain countries—such as

Macedonia, more than one-third of the workforce. Children at work may be harshly treated by their supervisors but at least they are kept off the far more menacing streets. Some kids even end up with a skill and are rendered employable.

VIEWPOINT 3

Bangladeshi Families Suffer Due to New Child Labor Laws

Evelyn Iritani

In the following viewpoint Evelyn Iritani asserts that, while some children in Bangladesh are benefitting from the crackdown on child labor and are able to attend school, others along with their families have been thrown into a worse situation—unable to work at relatively good jobs in the billion-dollar clothing industry and forced into harsher labor, or even employment as prostitutes. In acceding to American wishes by ending most child labor, Bangladeshi officials hoped that the United States would reward such good behavior monetarily, but instead, Iritani points out, a majority of American aid money has gone to other countries and the people of Bangladesh have suffered. Evelyn Iritani has served as a business reporter for the Los Angeles Times. *She won a Pulitzer Prize for national reporting in 2004.*

As you read, consider the following questions:

1. Why does the program that ended mainstream child labor in Bangladesh not feel like a success to many people there?

2. According to Iritani, what three elements have eroded Bangladeshi exports?

3. According to Iritani, how will an end to apparel quotas harm the Bangladeshi clothing industry even more?

Evelyn Iritani, "Child Labor Rules Don't Ease Burden in Bangladesh," *Los Angeles Times*, May 4, 2003, p. C1. Copyright © 2003 *Los Angeles Times*. Reproduced by permission.

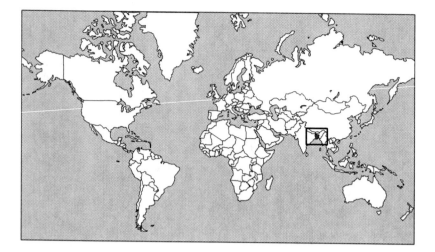

Three years ago, when Salma was 11, she worked in a Dhaka factory from 8 a.m. to 5 p.m., six days a week. She was a runner, trimming thread and shuttling bundles of sewn cloth. She made $9 a month.

Today [in 2003], the soft-spoken teenager is learning to read and write. Her parents are unhappy that she isn't bringing home wages, but they let her attend school because her teacher promised to help her find work soon that pays more than she earned at the factory.

"I hope to get a job making televisions," said Salma, sitting on the floor of a tidy, one-room schoolhouse where she and her classmates, a swarm of colorful saris and T-shirts, attended to their math workbooks.

Salma's climb from child laborer to dutiful student is a tribute to the Bangladesh Garment Manufacturers & Exporters Assn., which pledged eight years ago to remove children younger than 14 from factory floors.

Is Eliminating Child Labor a Success?

Under the association's program, designed in 1995 at the urging of the United States, the apparel industry has all but wiped out child labor. What's more, garment makers have sent nearly

10,000 children who once toiled in their factories to school, a considerable accomplishment in a country in which 35% don't make it past primary grades.

But to many people here, the program doesn't feel like much of a success.

Garment makers have sent nearly 10,000 children who once toiled in their factories to school, a considerable accomplishment in a country in which 35% don't make it past primary grades.

Although the garment industry satisfied U.S. demands for reform, the United States is buying fewer clothes from Bangladesh, which depends on apparel exports for three-fourths of its vital foreign-exchange dollars.

What's more, the [George W.] Bush administration this year added the predominantly Muslim country to its list of 34 nations whose citizens must navigate a rigorous visa application process in a program aimed at combating terrorism. That makes it difficult for businesspeople to visit customers and attend trade shows in the United States, the second-biggest buyer of Bangladeshi apparel after the European Union.

Politicians and businesspeople in the South Asian nation are bewildered—or suspect the worst: that the U.S. foreign policy establishment, focused on Iraq, Afghanistan and elsewhere, simply has forgotten about them.

Bangladeshi Industry Is in Trouble

"On child labor, Bangladesh responded in a major way; it was not window dressing," said Zulfiquar Rahman, managing director of Greenland Garments Ltd., which recently invested $1.4 million in a factory that produces clothing for several large European firms.

"In this case, we did get off our backsides and made things work, and I do not think it has been reciprocated."

Farooq Sobhan, a former top Bangladeshi official who teaches at George Washington University, said his countrymen watched the war in Iraq with particular interest.

"There's a lot of talk about rebuilding Iraq and making it into a functioning democracy," Sobhan said. "What about helping those countries which are already doing well to ensure that they remain democracies?"

Bangladesh has been a struggling democracy since 1971, when the Bengali-speaking portion of Pakistan launched a successful revolt against the Pakistani army. The small country on the Bay of Bengal, one of the most densely populated regions in the world, has been prone to disasters and always desperately poor, with 34% of its population living below the poverty line.

The United States buys about 40% of the $4.5 billion in apparel exported by Bangladesh, helping to turn the country into one of the world's largest producers of men's dress shirts and khaki pants.

And now the apparel industry, which employs 1.5 million of the country's 133 million people, is in trouble: Exports have been eroded by the global economic downturn, the rise of China as a garment manufacturer and, most stingingly, changing U.S. trade policies.

The United States buys about 40% of the $4.5 billion in apparel exported by Bangladesh, helping to turn the country into one of the world's largest producers of men's dress shirts and khaki pants.

After the Sept. 11 [2001] terrorist attacks, U.S. retailers reduced their orders, and today they are paying 30% to 50% less for shirts, slacks and other items, as weak global demand has driven down prices. The consequence: Companies in Bangladesh have eliminated 300,000 jobs and closed 1,200 factories, most of them in [the cities of] Dhaka and Chittagong, the major port.

But more than economic fundamentals are hurting Bangladeshi apparel companies. In 2002, the United States began giving special trade preferences to African, Andean and Caribbean apparel manufacturers. A U.S. company that buys a pair of slacks or a blouse from Bangladesh pays a tariff that is 8% to 30% higher than if it came from, say, Uganda or Peru.

The U.S. government says Bangladesh is such a world-class apparel producer that it doesn't need special treatment. That's hardly solace to the leaders of a country in which at least 35% of adults are unemployed and the per-capita annual income of $370 is one of the lowest in the world.

The Demise of Child Labor

Like other developing countries, Bangladesh catapulted into the global economy on the back of its cheap, plentiful labor force. During the 1980s, the apparel industry here ballooned as entrepreneurs turned dilapidated multistory buildings into sweatshops, many without ventilation or fire escapes. Workers, mostly young women and girls, migrated to the cities and toiled from dawn to nightfall. They earned a few pennies an hour, but that was more than they could make in the fields or cleaning house.

By the mid-1990s, labor activists estimated that as many as 50,000 children were helping to sew clothes for U.S. retailers such as Wal-Mart Stores Inc. and Kmart Corp.

Media exposés sparked the threat of a consumer boycott in the United States. Sen. Tom Harkin (D-Iowa) proposed prohibiting the import of any manufactured or mined goods made by children under age 15.

Threatened with the loss of its second-largest market, the Bangladeshi garment association signed a landmark child labor pact with the United Nations' International Labor Organi-

Percentages of Bangladeshi Working Children by Major Occupations

Occupation	Urban				Rural			
	Boys		Girls		Boys		Girls	
	Younger	Older	Younger	Older	Younger	Older	Younger	Older
Farmworker	0.00	3.81	0.00	0.00	38.75	55.40	6.67	29.63
Fisherman	0.00	1.90	0.00	0.00	6.25	5.83	6.67	3.70
Forest and livestock worker	0.00	0.00	0.00	0.00	10.00	2.04	0.00	0.00
Servant/maid	21.05	12.38	68.75	43.18	13.75	7.00	53.33	40.74
Salesman/businessman	52.63	29.53	0.00	0.00	12.50	12.83	6.67	3.70
Production worker	15.79	21.90	25.00	43.18	5.00	7.00	6.67	3.70
Transport/communication worker	5.26	7.62	0.00	0.00	2.50	1.46	0.00	0.00
Day laborer	5.26	2.86	0.00	0.00	5.00	1.46	0.00	0.00
Other	0.01	20.00	6.25	13.64	6.25	6.98	19.99	18.53
Total	100.00	100.00	100.00	100.00	100.00	100.00	100.00	100.00

TAKEN FROM: Shahina Amin, M. Shakil Quayes, and Janet M. Rives, "Poverty and Other Determinants of Child Labor in Bangladesh," *Southern Economic Journal*, April 2004.

zation and UNICEF [United Nations Children's Fund] on July 4, 1995. Not only would manufacturers stop employing children younger than 14, but the factories also would pay to have former child laborers educated. And parents would be given about $5 a month to offset the loss of a child's earnings.

So now, Salma and her 12-year-old sister spend their mornings studying in a schoolhouse in a crowded slum in the shadow of Dhaka's downtown office buildings. When asked a question, the shy teenager hides her face behind her silky red sari, barely speaking above a whisper. Her favorite subjects? "English and math."

Salma describes herself as lucky.

In the alley just outside her schoolroom, young girls beat rocks with large hammers, breaking off chunks that will be used to make bricks. They are wearing padded gloves, their faces covered with scarves. For their backbreaking labor, they will earn 10 to 20 taka—18 to 35 cents—a day.

[Critics of child labor legislation] say many young former factory workers ended up in far more dangerous jobs, including prostitution, because their families depend on their wages for survival.

There is no way of knowing whether these girls might have found less-taxing work in an apparel factory if the child labor agreement hadn't been forged. But critics of the pact call it a well-intentioned failure. They say many young former factory workers ended up in far more dangerous jobs, including prostitution, because their families depend on their wages for survival.

"One girl told me, 'I was earning 2,200 taka [$39] at the garment factory and I was helping my seven-member family survive. Please give my job back,'" said Mashuda Khatun Shefali, executive director of the Centre for Women's Initiatives, a Dhaka social services organization. "That is the reality."

The U.S. Defends the Program

In Washington, government officials consider the child labor project a model; the United States has helped establish similar programs in Pakistan's rug and soccer ball industries. A Labor Department spokesman said Bangladeshi factory owners were pioneers in the global battle against child labor and should be "applauded for their efforts."

But the United States never made any quid pro quo promises to Bangladesh, the spokesman said, adding that giving it beneficial trade status is a "matter for Congress."

To Bangladeshis, it sounds as if even its friends in Washington are passing the buck.

Harkin said the opposite is true. A spokesman for the senator said it was up to the Bush administration to decide whether—and how—Bangladesh should be rewarded for the "great job" it has done in all but eliminating children from apparel factory floors.

To Bangladeshis, it sounds as if even its friends in Washington are passing the buck.

"Unless you do something grossly and basically wrong, such as enter a nuclear race or an arms race, you are not recognized," said Bangladeshi Foreign Minister M. Morshed Khan.

Edward Gresser, director of trade and global markets at the Progressive Policy Institute in Washington, said the United States had inadvertently worsened the economic situation for Bangladesh and other Muslim countries by giving special trade benefits to non-Muslim countries.

He warned that the effect would be "to enlarge an already daunting pool of unemployable urban young people in the Muslim world, those most likely to be vulnerable to appeals from religious fundamentalists and terrorist groups."

U.S. officials say they are not ignoring Muslim economies, pointing to a free-trade pact the United States has with Jordan and a proposed agreement with Morocco. Bangladesh received $84 million in U.S. nonmilitary aid in 2002, compared with Pakistan's $625 million.

A Fierce Battle for the Apparel Market

In the United States, the powerful domestic textile and apparel manufacturing lobby has fought hard to protect the dwindling U.S. manufacturing base from low-cost imports. The American Textile Manufacturers Institute lobbied against proposals by American and foreign officials that allies in the U.S.-led war on terrorism—including Bangladesh, Pakistan and Turkey—be given preferential access to U.S. apparel markets.

"You shouldn't use the U.S. textile industry as a bargaining chip with Muslim countries," said Cass Johnson, a spokesman for the manufacturers group.

Other industrialized countries have responded to Bangladesh's plight: Japan, Canada and Australia recently joined the EU [European Union] in agreeing to provide quota-free and duty-free access with some restrictions for apparel products from the country.

"We want to save this business—otherwise we can't have jobs, we can't have workers rights."

But Bangladeshis fear that any gains will be obliterated in 2005, when the United States and other importing countries are scheduled to eliminate all apparel quotas. Once imports from China and India are no longer restricted, the contest for the lucrative U.S. market will be all the more fierce.

With the industry in Bangladesh caught by growing competition, falling prices and demands for higher labor standards, even longtime critics have become allies of apparel makers.

"The U.S. must consider something for the poor people," said Nazma Akter, a former child laborer who co-founded the

Bangladesh Independent Garment Workers Union Federation. "We want to save this business—otherwise we can't have jobs, we can't have workers rights."

Child Labor Is a Necessary Step on the Way to National Prosperity

Radley Balko

In the following viewpoint, Radley Balko states that liberals in civilized, developed countries tend to feel troubled about child labor in third world sweatshops, but the reality is that these workers and their parents are often quite comfortable, even happy with the conditions, so long as the jobs benefit them. Balko explains that history shows that every major industrialized country has gone through a period where child labor and sweatshops sustained economic growth, and countries such as India that historically resisted foreign investments and sweatshops have tended to stagnate economically. Unpleasant as it is for Westerners to think about children laboring in poor working conditions, Balko claims, the reality is that such circumstances are important for developing countries' economic maturation. Radley Balko has served as senior editor at Reason *magazine. He was a policy analyst for the Cato Institute, specializing in vice and civil liberties issues. He is also a columnist for* Fox News, *and his work has been published in the* Wall Street Journal, Forbes, Time, *and other newspapers and magazines.*

Radley Balko, "'Sweatshops,' Boycotts, and the Road to Poverty," *Capitalism Magazine* (Freeport, The Bahamas), May 11, 2003. www.capmag.com. Reproduced by permission.

As you read, consider the following questions:

1. How did the *New York Times* reporters' opinions on child labor and sweatshops change after their conversation with Mongkol Latlakorn? Why?

2. According to Balko, what choice did children have in nations like the United States and Britain during industrial periods?

3. In Balko's view, who is punished as a result or boycotts, fair trade regulations, and public pressure?

Two reporters relay this anecdote from Thailand:

> One of the half-dozen men and women sitting on a bench eating was a sinewy, bare-chested laborer in his late 30's named Mongkol Latlakorn. It was a hot, lazy day, and so we started chatting idly about the food and, eventually, our families. Mongkol mentioned that his daughter, Darin, was 15, and his voice softened as he spoke of her. She was beautiful and smart, and her father's hopes rested on her.
>
> "Is she in school?" we asked.
>
> "Oh, no," Mongkol said, his eyes sparkling with amusement. "She's working in a factory in Bangkok. She's making clothing for export to America." He explained that she was paid $2 a day for a nine-hour shift, six days a week.
>
> "It's dangerous work," Mongkol added. "Twice the needles went right through her hands. But the managers bandaged up her hands, and both times she got better again and went back to work."
>
> "How terrible," we murmured sympathetically.

So begins Nicholas Kristof and Sheryl WuDunn's article on sweatshops for the *New York Times* a few years ago. The two had lived off and on in Asia for 14 years, and were researching their upcoming book on emerging Asian economies, *Thunder from the East*. Like most westerners, Kristof and Wu-Dunn arrived in Asia horrified by the sweatshop conditions they'd heard about and witnessed. Like most Westerners—accustomed to 40-max-hour workweeks, sick leave, and vacation—the two were outraged at the way western companies exploited third world labor. But read on:

> Mongkol looked up, puzzled. "It's good pay," he said. "I hope she can keep that job. There's all this talk about factories closing now, and she said there are rumors that her factory might close. I hope that doesn't happen. I don't know what she would do then."

Mongkol's story illustrates how, by the time they wrote their book, Kristof and WuDunn had significantly upgraded their opinion of sweatshops. While regrettable, they concluded, sweatshops are a crucial and necessary step in most economies' evolution to prosperity.

Bans and Boycotts Can Be Harmful

Kristoff and WuDunn are right, of course. And efforts to ban, boycott, or otherwise shut down third world factories bring nothing but harm to the people they employ. Removing the best of a handful of bad options doesn't benefit the poor at all. It hurts them. And sometimes it kills them. Examples abound:

• In the early 1990s, the United States Congress considered the "Child Labor Deterrence Act," which would have taken punitive action against companies benefiting from child labor. The Act never passed, but the public debate it triggered put enormous pressure on a number of multinational corporations with assets in the U.S. One German garment maker laid off 50,000 child workers in Bangladesh. The British charity organization Oxfam later conducted a study that found that thousands of those laid-off children later became prostitutes, turned to crime, or starved to death.

• The United Nations organization UNICEF [United Nations Children's Fund] reports that an international boycott of the Nepalese carpet industry in the mid-1990s caused several plants to shut down; thousands of Nepalese girls later entered the sex trade.

• In 1995, a consortium of anti-sweatshop groups threw the spotlight on football (soccer) stitching plants in Pakistan. In response, Nike and Reebok shut down their plants in Pakistan, and several other companies followed suit. The result: tens of thousands of unemployed Pakistanis. Mean income in Pakistan fell by 20%. According to University of Colorado economist Keith E. Maskus, studies later showed a large proportion of those laid off ended up in crime, begging, or working as prostitutes.

• In 2000 the BBC [British Broadcasting Corporation] did an expose on sweatshop factories in Cambodia with ties to both Nike and the Gap. The BBC uncovered unsavory working conditions, and found several examples of children under 15 years of age working 12 or more hour shifts. After the BBC expose aired, both Nike and the Gap pulled out of Cambodia under public pressure. Cambodia lost $10 million in contracts, and hundreds of Cambodians lost their jobs.

Efforts to ban, boycott, or otherwise shut down third world factories bring nothing but harm to the people they employ.

How Free Trade Beats Sweatshops

In truth, every prosperous country on the planet today went through an industrial period heavily reliant on sweatshop labor. The United States, Britain, France, Sweden and others all rode to modernity on the backs of child laborers. The choice was simple: kids worked, or they went hungry. It wasn't a terribly rosy set of choices, but at least the choice was available.

Anti-globalization activists are doing their damndest to make sure choice *isn't* available to those living in today's fledgling economies.

Critics counter that unlike in the early 20th century, western companies today are wealthy enough to pay "living" wages, to establish comfortable working conditions, and to protect third world environments. They may be right.

But then, what advantage would there be to investing in the developing world in the first place? Cheap labor is the only chit the third world has to lure much-needed western investment. Take it away, and there's no reason for western corporations to incur the costs of putting up factories, shipping, security and the bevy of other expenses that come with maintaining plants overseas.

In truth, every prosperous country on the planet today went through an industrial period heavily reliant on sweatshop labor.

One of free trade's chief critics admits as much. In the introduction to his book *The Race to the Bottom*, anti-globalization icon Alan Tonelson writes the following, in reference to the World Trade Organization:

> Most of the organization's third world members—or at least their governments—opposed including any labor rights and environmental protections in trade agreements. They viewed low wages and lax pollution control laws as major assets they could offer to international investors—prime lures for job-creating factories and the capital they so desperately needed for other development-related purposes. Indeed, they observed, most rich countries ignored the environment and limited workers' power (to put it kindly) early in their economic histories. Why should today's developing countries be held to higher standards?

Tonelson, of course, was on his way to making another point. But he inadvertently revealed an inconsistency that will always plague the legitimacy of anti-globalist logic: boycotts, "fair trade" regulations and public pressure do nothing to punish the corporations who benefit from sweatshops. They punish only third world laborers and, to a lesser extent, western consumers.

The best way to lessen the plight of sweatshop workers is more free trade, not less. If workers make 75 cents per day in factory A—the only plant in town—the best thing that could happen to them would be for a second factory to open up. If Factory B pays less than 75 cents, it won't attract any workers. If it offers exactly 75 cents, it might attract a few workers who couldn't get jobs at factory A. If it pays more than 75 cents, however, it might attract the best and brightest from factory A. Factory A then must decide whether to up its wages, or look for new labor—which means more jobs.

The alternative: force factory A to pay artificially high wages. That negates the advantage factory A had by investing in a developing country in the first place. Factory A packs up and returns to the U.S. Factory B never happens, because factory B's parent company sees no advantage (see: cheap labor) in investing in the developing country. Factory A's workers' wages go from 75 cents per day to nothing.

The best way to lessen the plight of sweatshop workers is more free trade, not less.

Instead of two factories paying twice as many workers higher wages, enabling them to inch their way out of poverty, a community is left with no factories, no jobs, and no hope.

Examples of Sweatshop Success

Recent history teems with examples of how sweatshop labor has helped poor economies leap to prosperity. And given the

Progressive Labor Laws Do Not End Child Labor

[Let's consider] child labor. Most lefties and your kid's social-studies textbooks will tell you that child labor ended when progressives made it illegal. The truth is that child labor in America was almost gone when the government banned it. You can only make child labor illegal when enough parents are rich enough to no longer see the utility in putting the wee ones to work. That pattern is playing itself out across the globe today.

Jonah Goldberg, "Benign Neglect,"
National Review Online, *June 20, 2001.*
www.nationalreview.com.

interconnectivity and technology available in the current world economy—and that there's lots of western wealth to help them along—they can make the leap in a fraction of the time it took the west.

Kristoff and WuDunn note, for example, that it took Britain 58 years to double per capita GDP [gross domestic product] after its industrial revolution. China—home to millions of sweatshop workers—doubles its per capita GDP every ten years. In the sweatshop-dotted southern province of Dongguan, wages have increased fivefold in just the last few years. "A private housing market has appeared," Kristof and WuDunn write, "and video arcades and computer schools have opened to cater to workers with rising incomes. . . . A hint of a middle class has appeared."

If China's provinces were separate countries, the two authors write, the 20 fastest growing economies from 1978 to 1995 would all have been Chinese.

Swedish economist Johan Norberg writes in his book *In Defense of Global Capitalism* that where it took Sweden 80 years to reach modernity, it has taken Taiwan and Hong Kong just 25. He predicts that all of South and East Asia will be prosperous enough to ban child labor entirely by 2010.

But that's just it. A country must be able to *afford* to ban child labor before child labor is pulled out from under it. Otherwise, without work, the children there beg, or starve, or die of malaria, or diarrhea.

China, Taiwan, Hong Kong—all accepted sweatshop labor as an unsavory stepping stone to prosperity.

Good Intentions and the Road to Poverty

Contrast those nations to the countries that have traditionally been "spared" sweatshops: the results are striking.

India, for example, has long resisted allowing itself to be "exploited" by foreign investment. It was one of the last major countries in the world to be introduced to Coca-Cola. Consequently, India festered in abject poverty for decades. India has only opened its markets to the west in the latter part of the last century and, as Norberg writes, its economy immediately showed signs of life. India's percentage of child laborers in the workforce has fallen from 35% to just 12%.

The economist and syndicated columnist Thomas Sowell describes how anti-sweatshop sentiments in the 1950s hindered progress in West Africa:

Half a century ago, public opinion in Britain caused British firms in colonial West Africa to pay higher wages than local economic conditions would have warranted. Net result? Vastly more job applicants than jobs.

Not only did great numbers of frustrated Africans not get jobs. They did not get the work experience that would have allowed them to upgrade their skills and become more valuable and higher-paid workers later on.

Today, of course, western and sub-Saharan Africa are among the most destitute regions on earth. Per capita GDP there is actually *lower* today than it was in the 1960s.

But even within that desolation, there flicker faint glimmers of hope. Norberg writes that a few countries—Botswana, Ghana, and most notably Uganda—have liberalized their trade policies in recent years and have already seen double-digit decreases in poverty rates. One wonders what might have happened if well-intentioned public opinion in 1950s Britain could have stomached the short-term discomfort of early industrialization in Africa for the long-term benefits of modernized economies. Today's Africa may have been much, much different.

Third world governments welcome sweatshop. Most third world laborers welcome them too.

The Debate Goes On

In the end, it's perfectly natural and acceptable for comfortable western consumers to feel unsettled about sweatshops overseas. Modest public pressure on companies might even help to lessen the burden borne by third world economies in transition. But boycotting sweatshops—or lobbying for laws at home that enforce "living wages" overseas—rob developing countries of their competitive advantage over western markets.

Third world governments welcome sweatshops. Most third world laborers welcome them, too. History has shown that they're important for the maturation of developing economies. Western consumers win cheaper goods. It seems the only losers here are anti-globalization activists and organized labor groups unable to compete with cheaper workforces overseas. On balance, the clear winners in the sweatshop debate seem clear.

Periodical Bibliography

Douglass Clement   "Why Johnny Can't Work," *Region*, vol. 19, no. 2, June 2005, pp. 32–40.

Sylvain Dessy and John Knowles   "Why Is Child Labor Illegal?" *European Economic Review*, October 2008.

The Economist   "Sickness or Symptom?" February 7, 2004.

Andrew W. Horowitz and Julie R. Trivitt   "Does Child Labor Reduce Youth Crime?" *KYKLOS*, November 2007.

Jillian Lloyd   "Child-Labor Twist: Town Favors Kids Working," *Christian Science Monitor*, February 8, 2000.

Hugh A. McCabe   "Hiring Minors: It's Not as Easy as You Think," *San Diego Business Journal*, June 28, 2004.

David Montero   "Nike's Dilemma: Is Doing the Right Thing Wrong?" *Christian Science Monitor*, December 22, 2006.

Charles M. North and Bob Smietana   "Shopping for Justice: The Trouble with Good Intentions," *The Christian Century*, March 11, 2008.

John J. Tierney Jr.   "The World of Child Labor," *The World & I Online*, vol. 15, August 2000, p. 54.

CHAPTER 4

Efforts to End Child Labor Around the World

"Mainstreaming" Is a Successful Approach to Ending Child Labor

International Labour Organization

"Mainstreaming" is a strategy for eliminating child labor by attacking the problem as part of a larger political, social, and economic strategy. Mainstreaming seeks to reduce the supply of child workers as well as to eliminate the need for such workers. In the following viewpoint, the International Labour Organization (ILO) explains its efforts to enact mainstreaming through a four-point plan, including: 1) "improving the knowledge base" by broadening understanding of the problem through data collection and assessment; 2) "advocacy" for anti-child labor efforts by raising awareness; 3) "capacity building" to strengthen the power of organizations that seek an end to child labor; and 4) "policy development and coordination," through which anti-child labor laws will be enforced on a national and global scale. The International Labour Organization of the United Nations deals with labor issues. It is located in Geneva, Switzerland.

As you read, consider the following questions:

1. According to the ILO, upon what three premises are its campaign against child labor based?

2. Through what four main fronts will the ILO attack child labor on a global scale?

International Labour Organization, *The End of Child Labor: Within Reach*, Geneva, Switzerland: International Labour Office, 2006, pp. 53–56. Reproduced by permission.

3. In the article, what is meant by "capacity building"?

It is now widely recognized that targeted interventions to withdraw, rehabilitate and reintegrate child labourers have their role for specific populations of children, and that many of these interventions can and must be scaled up. However, the effective abolition of child labour on a national scale is only feasible if countries succeed in diminishing the poverty dimension of the problem and if, at the same time, they take a variety of other measures to reduce exclusion and discrimination. This realization is based essentially on three premises:

the massive scale of the problem, making interventions by an intergovernmental organization or other outside actor on a very wide scale unproductive;

the intimate links between the elimination of child labour and various other dimensions of development; and

the principle that prevention is better than cure.

Mainstreaming of child labour concerns [isl the key strategy to raising the profile of the issue and to ensuring greater impact.

Fortunately, development efforts in many countries are now being channelled within the context of various complementary frameworks such as the Millennium Development Goals (MDGs), the Poverty Reduction Strategy Papers (PRSPs) process, the Education For All (EFA) initiative, the ILO's Decent Work Agenda and—specific to Africa—the New Partnership for Africa's Development (NEPAD). Varying in focus—on the promotion of pro-poor growth strategies, expansion of educational opportunities, and extension of social protection to the most vulnerable groups—such frameworks constitute ideal vehicles for combating child labour, attacking its structural determinants and creating alternatives. The main theme of this section is on mainstreaming of child labour concerns as the key strategy to raising the profile of the issue and to ensuring greater impact.

A Worldwide Effort

The principal focus of mainstreaming efforts should clearly be at the national level. This is where the main policies affecting child labour are formulated, decisions regarding resource allocation are made, and the final impact of action against child labour is assessed. The primary role of the international community is to assist national authorities in their mainstreaming efforts. But mainstreaming can also be fruitful, and indeed is essential, at the international level, in the form of the worldwide movement against child labour, as part of efforts to create a conducive environment for more effective action at the national and local levels.

Mainstreaming requires action on many fronts, which may usefully be grouped under four main headings: (i) improving the knowledge base; (ii) advocacy; (iii) capacity building; and (iv) policy development and coordination.

Improving the Knowledge Base

Empirical evidence on child labour and the analysis of its links to other aspects of development are crucial in informing discussions about mainstreaming efforts, broadening the support base for the integration of child labour concerns in policy formulation, and facilitating this integration. But although IPEC [International Programme on the Elimination of Child Labour] has been working actively to improve coverage, this evidence is underdeveloped globally.

The main reason for the relative paucity of statistical data on child labour is the low priority it tended to receive in the past. If the elimination of child labour were to become a more fully mainstreamed development objective, it would attract the necessary resources to fill the gap. To some extent this is already happening. A number of countries have carried out child labour surveys on their own or, in most cases, with the assistance of the ILO [International Labour Organization] or other international organizations. A variety of other types of survey are also being carried out that provide relevant information for child labour analysis, such as UNICEF's [United Nations Children's Fund's] Multiple Indicator Cluster Surveys (MICS) and the Living Standards Measurement Study (LSMS) surveys of the World Bank. Furthermore, the data sets from these surveys are in most cases made available through the Internet to encourage their use and further analysis. The number of such surveys is still limited, however, and few countries have carried out more than one to allow for assessment of changes over time.

In regard to analytical work, the first priority should be to highlight the links, often running both ways, between child labour and the principal objectives of the policy processes into which it is to be integrated. These include poverty reduction of course, but also the development of human resources, universal primary education, economic growth, labour productivity, wage policy, income distribution and population growth and dynamics, as well as more intangible objectives such as improving the country's image abroad. The results of such work would not only improve the knowledge base on child labour, they would also serve as a powerful means of convincing policy makers of the importance of greater attention to child labour.

Another important priority in analytical work should be to assess the implications for child labour of the principal policy measures proposed and how their impact may be made more positive from the child labour standpoint. Analytical questions of interest with regard to poverty reduction strategies include, for example, whether the proposed strategy is able to reach child labour households, easing their income constraints through provision of greater opportunities for productive employment and income-generating activities. Are these households targeted in any way as a priority group? Will any proposed reforms of the education system ensure affordable access to quality schooling to *all* children, including child labourers? Are adequate economic incentives envisaged and budgeted to encourage parents to send their children to school and keep them there? Is the proposed strategy compatible with existing child labour legislation, policies and programmes? Is there any coordination with existing interventions, such as a Time-Bound Programme (TBP) for the elimination of the worst forms of child labour, and do they complement each other?

The question of who should undertake such efforts aimed at the generation of knowledge and its dissemination is an important one. Ideally, in each country a child labour knowledge network would be in place. This is unfortunately not yet the case in most countries. Capable research institutions exist in many developing countries that make an enormous contribution to the better understanding of socio-economic phenomena, but child labour is not often on their agenda.

The main reason for the relative paucity of statistical data on child labour is the low priority it tended to receive in the past.

Advocacy

It is not surprising that child labour has a low profile in the policy process at the national and international levels. The poor have the weakest voice and their capacity for social action in a hostile political environment is limited. Advocacy efforts are therefore an indispensable tool, and there are many entry points for raising child labour concerns.

There is a need to continue to raise awareness about child labour, its nature and extent, its determinants, links to poverty

What Is Mainstreaming?

Broadly speaking, the term "mainstreaming" refers to concerted efforts to influence processes, policies and programmes that have a significant bearing on child labour elimination. It may be seen in some ways as analogous to the concept of gender mainstreaming that has evolved over the years and witnessed considerable success. Adapting an official definition of gender mainstreaming by the United Nations Economic and Social Council (ECOSOC), child labour mainstreaming may be more formally defined as:

the process of assessing the implications for child labourers, or those at risk of becoming child labourers, of any planned action, including legislation, policies or programmes, in any area and at all levels;

a strategy for making the concerns about child labour an integral part of the design, implementation, monitoring and evaluation of policies and programmes in all political, economic, and societal spheres, so as to reduce both the supply of and demand for child labour, especially in its worst forms; and

a process whose ultimate goal is the total elimination of child labour as soon as possible.

H. Tabatabai: "Mainstreaming Action Against Child Labour in Development and Poverty Reduction Strategies," Time-Bound Programme Manual for Action Planning, *International Labour Organization, 2003.*

and the labour market, education, economic and social implications, population structure and dynamics, and its potential to act as an obstacle to and retard long-term development. It is also necessary to promote the elimination of child labour as an explicit development objective, and as a part of a poverty reduction strategy. In addition, the growing prominence of child labour concerns has now created an environment in which the formation of child labour constituencies is made easier than in the past. There is a need to take advantage of the current momentum to build such constituencies where they do not exist and strengthen them where they do, through active involvement in existing participatory processes (such as PRSPs and the United Nations Development Assistance Framework [UNDAF], etc.), building alliances with the civil society groups most concerned.

A growing number of countries are moving towards the formulation of a national policy on child labour.

Capacity Building

There is a need to strengthen the technical, organizational and managerial capacity of various child labour stakeholders, in particular ILO constituents, as well as NGOs [non-governmental organizations], through upgrading their technical expertise and the promotion of alliances among them. The formulation of national strategies for development and poverty reduction and the integration of child labour concerns in them involve many technical issues, but they are fundamentally political processes through which competing objectives, approaches and interests are resolved before national priorities are identified. Objectives and approaches that do not enjoy the support of sufficiently strong constituencies are bound to receive lower priority in the national agenda. One reason why child labour is not high on the development agenda is that such constituencies have so far been largely lacking or weak, both at the national and international levels. Within the government, the ministry or ministries responsible for child labour issues are often among the weakest politically and, as a consequence, technically as well. Similarly, international development frameworks such as the MDGs and PRSPs do not adequately accommodate child labour concerns.

Policy Development and Coordination

Comprehensive action against child labour involves a broad range of policies, programmes and projects, and thus many stakeholders in the public and private sectors. This poses a major challenge in terms of policy development and effective coordination among various state and non-state actors.

Mainstreaming efforts would be considerably helped if comprehensive national child labour policies and action programmes already existed. Article 1 of Convention No. 138 [a 1973 international treaty on child labor] requires ratifying member States "to pursue a national policy designed to ensure the effective abolition of child labour". Paragraph 1 of the accompanying Recommendation No. 146 provides guidance on the design of such a policy, noting in particular that "high priority should be given to planning for and meeting the needs of children and youth in national development policies and programmes and to the progressive extension of the interrelated measures necessary to provide the best possible conditions of physical and mental growth for children and young persons".

There are as yet few countries where this requirement has been translated into a clear, coherent and comprehensive statement of a national policy on child labour. With increasing ratification of Convention No. 138 (as indicated by the analysis of reports submitted to the Committee of Experts on the Application of Conventions and Recommendations), a growing number of countries are moving towards the formulation of a national policy on child labour, but this is not yet the case in a large number of countries.

Banning Child Labor Won't Solve the Problem

Amela Karabegovic and Jason Clemens

In the following viewpoint, Amela Karabegovic and Jason Clemens contend that the answer to the child labor problem does not lie in simply banning the practice, however attractive and simple that solution seems. Child labor is a deep-rooted problem that stems from poverty. But banning child labor does not improve the lot of poverty-stricken families, the authors assert. Instead, they claim improving economic conditions by promoting free trade is a more effective and long-lasting solution to eradicating the need for child labor. Amela Karabegovic is a research economist for the Fraser Institute, a Canadian research organization that promotes a free market economy. Jason Clemens is a director in the fiscal studies department at the Fraser Institute.

As you read, consider the following questions:

1. What did a UNICEF study of bans on child labor in Nepal reveal?

2. According to the authors, history has demonstrated that what four factors of economically free countries lead to the highest rates of prosperity?

3. How did Vietnamese children benefit as a result of free trade when rice prices rose, according to the authors?

Amela Karabegovic and Jason Clemens, "Ending Child Labour—Bans Aren't the Solution," *The Fraser Forum*, March 2005, pp. 25–26. Reprinted with permission from The Fraser Institute, http://www.fraserinstitute.org.

Child labour is an unfortunate reality in many of the world's poorer countries. We can all agree that ending it is a desirable goal. It is the means by which to achieve this end where disagreement exists. All too often the activists who pursue this cause are guided by their emotions. As a result, they frequently advocate policies that are intuitively appealing but which actually make matters worse, such as bans on child labour and reductions in free trade. Dispassionate, objective research indicates that only policies such as free trade, that improve parental productivity and thus incomes, will eliminate child labour—just as they did in western countries.

Parents in poorer countries, just like those in richer countries, do not want their children to have to work. The children work from necessity; their families are unable to generate sufficient income to survive with only the parents working due to low productivity and correspondingly low wages. A case study examining child labour in Bangladesh by Shahina Amin, Shakil Quayes, and Janet Rives published in the *Southern Economic Journal* confirmed this: "a family's poverty affects the probability that a child will work: keeping children away from work is a luxury these families cannot afford." An earlier review of child labour by Assefa Admassie for the African Development Bank agreed: "poverty is indeed one of the most important reasons for the high incidence of child labour in Africa."

Bans Often Make the Situation Worse

It will not help at all to simply ban child labour without dealing with the fundamental problem, which is a lack of productivity and income. In fact, such a ban will make matters worse. A study published in the *Economic Journal* in January 2005 by two Canadian academics, Sylvain Dessy and Stéphane Pallage investigated the effects of banning child labour, and in particular banning those jobs deemed to be the worst for children (defined as those that expose children to physical and psychological stresses). Unfortunately, their results indicate that even a "ban on the worst forms of child labour in poor countries is unlikely to be welfare improving." The researchers found that if child labour is banned, families would be unable to recoup the loss in family income, making them worse off. The researchers also found that the reduction in income that would result if children were prevented from working impeded the accumulation of human capital, which is essential for productivity improvements and ultimately wage gains.

Equally distressing is the finding that bans on child labour often lead to children working in the illegal or black market sector of the economy, often in dangerous conditions. Kaushik Basu and Zafiris Tzannatos completed a literature review on child labour for the *World Bank Economic Review*. "The Global Child Labor Problem: What Do We Know and What Can We Do?" specifically refers to a UNICEF [United Nations Children's Fund] study on bans on child labour in export industries in Nepal that have driven children into prostitution.

Parents in poorer countries, just like those in richer countries, do not want their children to have to work.

The implication from these studies seems clear: poorer countries and their citizens (including children) do not benefit from bans on child labour. Indeed, a 2003 paper published in the *Canadian Journal of Economics* by Sylvain Dessy and Désiré Vencatachellum concluded that, "Only rich countries and those that are not 'too' poor ... benefit from adopting child labour laws."

A Solution: Free Trade

What is the solution? Mahmood Hussain and Keith Maskus argue in *Child Labour Use and Economic Growth: An Econometric Analysis* that the ultimate solution to child labour is to increase the productivity and thus the incomes of parents. In

Bans Do Not Reduce Child Labor

Although ... trade policies have highlighted the issue of child labor on the political agenda, there are several problems in using them in practice. First, if these policies lead to trade sanctions that reduce average family income, they could potentially increase the incidence of child labor. On the other hand, if the sanctions are only implemented very rarely, then they will not be a credible threat. Second, the recent history of trade sanctions aimed to promote broader political change does not suggest much optimism about their efficacy. Third, it's not clear what specific action the trade pressures should be seeking to create. For example, preventing children from working in one high-profile job may do nothing more than force children to change employers—perhaps for the worse. Attempts to require either bans on child labor or compulsory school attendance are subject to the problems above. Fourth, it is difficult to distinguish whether these measures reflect genuine interest in the well-being of children in poor countries or whether they are just a palatable excuse for protectionism. Overall, it is difficult to make a strong case for trade policy or consumer boycotts as an effective tool to combat child labor. Consumer activism has brought the problem of child labor into the spotlight, but we are not aware of any systematic empirical evidence of the effectiveness of consumer activism in reducing child labor. It seems a blunt tool that is unlikely to reach the typical child laborer who helps parents on the family farm and in domestic chores.

Eric V. Edmonds and Nina Pavcnik, "Child Labor in the Global Economy," The Journal of Economic Perspectives, Winter 2005.

fact, the implication of almost every study cited in this article is the same: to eliminate child labour, societies must improve parental productivity and income. In short, the ultimate solution to child labour is to pursue and implement polices that lead to economic prosperity.

History has proven that economically free countries experience the highest rates of economic prosperity through the promotion of the rule of law, secure property rights, limited government, and free trade. These types of policies will increase parental earnings, which will ultimately enable them to offset the income losses associated with their children no longer working.

[Child labour] bans exacerbate the problems and may force families into worse living conditions and the children themselves into more dangerous employment.

Interestingly, a study of the Vietnamese economy by [Eric] Edmonds and [Nina] Pivcnik investigates how freer trade affected child labour in that country. The study concluded that rice prices rose when the market (both exports and imports) was opened to competition; the result was a decline in child labour from 57 percent in 1993 to 38 percent in 1998. Significantly, the percentage of children not attending school also declined. This is but one example of the beneficial effects of free trade.

While ending child labour is a laudable goal, simply banning it is not a solution. In fact, bans exacerbate the problems and may force families into worse living conditions and the children themselves into more dangerous employment. The real solution lies in the promotion of policies that lead to economic growth and prosperity. With an increase in family wealth, parents can afford to support their children, rather than asking the children to help support their families.

Campaigns to End Child Labor Should Focus on Sending Every Child to School

Gerard Oonk

In the following viewpoint, Gerard Oonk argues that child labor is inherently wrong and that all children must attend school. He seeks to broaden the focus of many child labor opponents who focus narrowly on the worst forms of child labor; instead, he feels that advocates should concentrate efforts on eliminating all child work. Most people blame child labor on poverty, but Oonk claims that poverty is not the determining factor in causing child labor. He believes that bureaucratic roadblocks often prevent poor parents from enrolling their children in schools. Gerard Oonk is the director of the India Committee of the Netherlands, a nongovernmental organization devoted to improving life for the most oppressed peoples of India. He gave this speech at the First Children's World Congress on Child Labour in Florence, Italy, in May 2004.

As you read, consider the following questions:

1. What examples does Oonk provide to show that poverty is not the only cause of child labor in Indian states?

2. What strategy does Oonk believe the school systems of India should adopt?

Gerard Oonk, "Stop Child Labour—School Is the Best Place to Work, speech given at the First Children's World Congress on Child Labour, Florence, Italy," India Committee of the Netherlands, May 2004. www.indianet.nl. Reproduced by permission.

3. According to Oonk, what roadblocks do the school systems impose that prevent poor parents from enrolling their children in school?

L et me start by first making two somewhat provocative statements.

One has already been made by Sonia Rosen [a previous speaker] and I want to elaborate a little bit on that, and that is: poverty is not the main cause of child labour.

The second is: the policy of governments and international donors is too much focused on the worst forms or the abusive forms of child labour instead of all child labour and the relation between education and child labour.

Poverty is not the main cause of child labour.

I'm saying that on behalf of the campaign "Stop Child Labour: School Is the Best Place to Work", a bit too long for a title for a campaign but, ok, let's call it Stop Child Labour. What this campaign is working at is to redefine the struggle against child labour in its relation to the right to full-time education, and to link that to the role of international donors like ILO [International Labour Organization], UNICEF [United Nations Children's Fund], World Bank, national governments, and so on.

Poverty Doesn't Necessarily Cause Child Labor

First the poverty issue. It's very remarkable that in two states of India, Kerala and Himachal Pradesh, states which are not so rich, most of the children are going to school and there is very little child labour. Of course children still do work after school but most of the children go to full time education. Well, a lot of people don't expect this because the general impression is: if you are a poor child in India you cannot go to school. This is not the case. There is a third state in India, Andhra Pradesh, where there is now a movement for the last ten years, led by the NGO [non-governmental organization] MV Foundation [an Indian child rights organization] which has brought about 250,000 poor children, mostly from agricultural labourers' and small farmers families, to school. Among these 250,000 are a lot of girls and boys tied up by so-called debt-induced bonded labour, in fact a form of slavery, as well as a lot of girls . . . who have been working long days in the households. So, that shows it is possible to bring poor children to school, by investing in education, by local mobilisation, by—of course—free education and—especially important—by establishing the social norm amongst communities that a child should be in school and not work.

The social norm has to be developed among people that it is not right for children to work.

I cannot enough stress the importance of this element. The social norm has to be developed among people that it is not right for children to work. What is happening in many instances where we target too much on specific forms of child labour is that we do condone a lot of other forms of child labour, which is also preventing children from attending full-time education. But the Convention on the rights of child[ren] is clear enough: any work that is either hazardous or interferes with the education of the child should be prohibited. So, the Convention does not talk about the worst forms of child labour alone, however important of course it is *to include* these children. Our contention as Stop Child Labour campaign is that you can in fact only reach those children who are in the worst forms of child labour if you address the whole population of child labourers. Otherwise you cannot create that social norm and you will pull out some children working in these worst forms and other children will be recruited, as is happening in many places today.

The Focus Must Be on All Child Laborers

So, our problems with policies of governments and international donors is that they [are] reinforcing the idea [that] some children can in fact not go to full-time education because they are too poor and have to work. Everybody agrees education is important and more money is needed and our campaign strongly supports that. However, donors often have no vision of how to deal with the issue of child labour as a part of, as an aspect of educational funding and policies.

What you often see is that the whole focus is on the infrastructure, on the quality of education, in the sense of providing school books, training teachers—which is all extremely important—but they forget about the population of out-of-school children, which for example in a country like India, but also in other countries, is quite large. So the school system itself has no strategy how to include out-of school children and does not feel responsible to bring those children into school which are now out of school. Thus the school system needs to do more than just providing education. On the other hand, child labour strategies often lack an entry point or link into the formal education system and do piece by piece projects on their own.

These are the issues we are trying to address and we are in fact saying there is too little linkage between the two elements of child labour and education. Take the Dakar framework of Action [a 2000 meeting in Senegal where a policy of education for all children was affirmed]: no mention of child labour. Take the World Bank, the major funder of education projects: they only talk about harmful child labour. Does that mean every child which is not in full-time education? I don't think so.

Barriers to Education

The barriers to education that generate exclusion may be grouped under the following categories:

Accessibility

- Physical remoteness and social barriers (e.g. girls' restricted freedom of movement), distance to school.
- Discrimination (e.g. based on region, gender, race, ethnicity, religion, caste, class, HIV/AIDS status).
- Burden of household chores on girls in the family home.
- Early marriage.
- Burden faced by children combining work and school.
- Lack of birth registration.
- Inflexible scheduling.
- Fear of violence at, and on the way to, school.

Affordability

- Direct costs (e.g. school fees, other compulsory fees).
- Indirect costs (e.g. uniforms, textbooks, transportation, meals).
- Opportunity cost (i.e. income/wage lost to family from child leaving work to go to school).

Quality

- Lack of infrastructure, facilities (such as separate water and sanitation facilities for girls), materials and support systems for children.
- Inadequate conditions of work for teachers (short-term contracts, heavy workloads, low pay, etc.).
- Low status of teachers.
- Lack of adequate training, aids and materials for teachers.
- Lack of female teachers, especially at secondary level.
- Lack of sensitivity of education authorities and teachers to the needs of children at risk of dropping out.

Relevance

- Curriculum detached from local language, needs, values and aspirations of children at risk of dropping out.
- Curriculum inadequate to prepare older children for the world of work through careers guidance, etc.

TAKEN FROM: International Labour Organization, *Combating Child Labor Through Education* Geneva, Switzerland: International Labour Organization, 2008.

All Children Must Attend School

So, in fact, coming back to the poverty argument there is a big lack of political will to bring children to school. There are a lot of indifferently, badly functioning schools. So, what can be done? What we suggest is the following: if educational funding is being put under conditions by these big donors, what they should do is not only fund education in terms of infrastructures and teachers etc., they should also fund those campaigns, those groups, those governments, those non-governmental organisations and trade unions which are doing social mobilisation to get all the children into school. Also, programmes should be supported to bring all those children, who are already for example 10–11 and missed the first grades, into school because that shows that we really care also about those children. We are not saying "leave those children by the way side, they are too old now and forget about them"—no, they should be brought to school as well. And one important point which I still want to make mention is that the whole bureaucracy of the school system itself pushes out a lot of, especially poor, children. The school system itself is often so insensitive to children by asking for birth certificates, medical certificates etc. It should be the responsibility of the school to help parents with it, while now it is very often the responsibility of poor illiterate parents who don't know how to deal with it. So, these kind of stupid, insensitive bureaucracies drive out a lot of poor children because they do not know how to deal with the school system as such. Helping children and their parents to overcome the bureaucratic hurdles of going to school should also be part of the education system. It should be part of the overall aim to bring every child to school.

Corporations Must Take Responsibility for Child Labor

Poulomi Saha and Tobias Webb

In the following viewpoint, Poulomi Saha and Tobias Webb contend that corporations must play a larger role in ending child labor in their supply chains. When informed that their products are made using child labor, corporations traditionally plead ignorance. But, the authors contend, corporations can take the lead in ending such practices by instituting creative practices and better safeguards against child labor. Creative companies such as IKEA have instituted better monitoring and have worked with locals to find ways to ensure that child labor laws are followed. Ingrained practices in countries such as India have perpetuated child labor, the authors explain, but new approaches and creative solutions can alter unsatisfactory traditions. Poulomi Saha writes about European and Asian news for Ethical Corporation *magazine, where she has served as India editor, Europe writer, and assistant editor. Tobias Webb is the founding editor of* Ethical Corporation *magazine, Ethicalcorp.com and Climate ChangeCorp.com. He is also co-director of the Ethical Corporation Institute, a research arm of* Ethical Corporation.

As you read, consider the following questions:

1. According to the article, why do corporations struggle to root out child labor in their supply chains?

Poulomi Saha and Tobias Webb, "Facing Up to the Child Labour Challenge: Tackling Supply Chain Child Labour Is Not an Impossible Task," *Ethical Corporation Magazine* (London), September, 2005, pp. 40–42. Copyright © *Ethical Corporation*. Reproduced by permission.

2. What new approaches are corporations such as IKEA using to tackle child labor issues?

3. What role do the authors believe non-governmental organizations can play in helping corporations work better with local governments to enforce child labor laws?

A recent report by Indian non-governmental organisations has again thrown light on the pandemic that is child labour in the country. "Our Mining Children", written by a fact-finding team from groups including the MV Foundation, Oxfam Swaraj and Campaign Against Child Labour, looks at the issue in India's mining sector, which employs an estimated one million children. The team found about 200,000 of them working in the Bellary district of Karnataka state.

According to the latest (2001) Indian census, out of 210 million children aged between five and 14, an estimated 11.2 million are working. This accounts for about 5% of the estimated 211 million children working in the world and more than half the number of child workers in the Asia-Pacific region.

According to the latest (2001) Indian census, out of 210 million children aged between five and 14, an estimated 11.2 million are working.

According to the new report, most of the children at Bellary's mines are involved in strenuous activities like digging and breaking stones. It says they are also engaged in the other processing activities of iron ore mining, without access to any safety equipment.

While the report heavily criticises companies employing child workers indirectly in their supply chains, a few companies are setting an example for the rest in tackling the problem.

Companies Must Take Responsibility

Many companies have been seen, when discovering that child labour exists in their supply chains, to have been ignorant of the local social and economic conditions among their suppliers. Key among these conditions are often thin profit margins in poor communities where children often have to work to support a subsistence living.

In the case of many unscrupulous (or desperate) farm and factory owners and managers, the low level of their revenues can lead to the employment of cheap labour in the form of children.

Child labour experts say companies should address this on a basic level by raising their suppliers' profit margins and pushing them to employ adults, using audits to verify progress. However, corporate insiders point out that in many nations, the use of child workers is almost institutionalised, ingrained in local cultures through years of poverty, poor education and lack of strict law enforcement systems.

NGOs [non-governmental organizations] often acknowledge this, and the fact that the culture of child labour existed before the sourcing of products by multinational companies from poorer nations. However, both sides generally agree nowadays that, morally and reputationally, this excuses no-one from taking action on this most emotive of issues.

Regular Monitoring Is a Key

Regular third-party monitoring and social audits of supplier premises are necessary to ensure that buyers' social and environmental standards are enforced, say labour standards experts.

Swedish home furnishings company IKEA has a strict code of conduct, says its ban on child labour is "non-negotiable" and makes suppliers sign up to the company's code of conduct to secure purchase orders.

IKEA requires all its suppliers to disclose all their production centres, which it then monitors through announced checks, while its auditors, KPMG, spring surprise inspections.

Factories found to be in violation of IKEA's code of conduct are put on probation for at least six months. During this time they are expected to put forward an action plan to ensure all child workers are placed in schools and that their education to the age of 14 is paid for. In some cases, suppliers are expected to compensate child workers' families for the income lost by placing them in schools. If all this is not done to the company's satisfaction, IKEA withdraws its business.

Complex Outcomes

Partnerships, says the International Labour Organisation [ILO], are imperative to finding collective solutions to the problem of child labour.

Back in the late 1990s, the organisation's International Programme on the Elimination of Child Labour had success in eliminating child labour in the soccer ball industry of Pakistan's Sialkot district with the help of local NGOs, the district government and the Sialkot Chamber of Commerce and Industry. With ILO training in operational, auditing and reporting standards, the local NGOs are now better equipped to monitor progress. However, in this case, the end result was not what some might have wanted.

Poverty is historically seen as the dominant cause of child labour in India. But this view is being increasingly challenged.

While child labour was virtually eliminated from the area's soccer ball production, that meant all workers had to be monitored. For cultural reasons, many women workers were not able to leave their houses and work in a monitored factory, and so lost their jobs. According to one source involved in the project, some 20,000 workers became unemployed so that child labour could be eliminated from the branded soccer ball industry in time for the 1998 World Cup.

To avert such an outcome, the India Committee of the Netherlands suggests companies should involve local community members or NGOs in the auditing and monitoring process. Locally known faces, used as part of the auditing process, can help win the confidence of workers, it says. The issue of homeworkers and associated problems of monitoring this informal economy is a well-acknowledged problem, but there are potential solutions beginning to emerge.

Poverty Is Not the Only Cause of Child Labor

Poverty is historically seen as the dominant cause of child labour in India. But this view is being increasingly challenged by NGOs such as the MV Foundation, which cites India's incompetently run education system as a principal challenge. Other barriers include bureaucratic hurdles for the poor to access and stay in schools, gender and caste discrimination and, more generally, the absence of a norm that children should not work but be in school.

Such systemic problems, the NGO says, can be overcome when people are confident that their local school is functioning. Today, as a result of the foundation's work, 700 villages in India's Andhra Pradesh state are child-labour-free and 320,000 children have moved from work to school.

UNICEF, the United Nations Children's Fund, has collaborated with IKEA to address some of these challenges in the carpet industry of India's Uttar Pradesh state.

IKEA finances UNICEF initiatives that aim to improve the educational infrastructure in communities and help children get back to school. Among these are "alternative learning centres" or "bridge schools" that aim to help older children who have lost study years through work to catch up with others of their age within 18–24 months. IKEA has invested about $1.5 million over a seven-year period towards these initiatives. Another $270,000 has been dedicated towards various health programmes run by UNICEF and the World Health Organisation [WHO] to ensure children do not skip school because of ailments.

A New Approach

Though not bonded labourers per se, most children in Uttar Pradesh's carpet industry are compelled to work in order to repay debts taken by their parents from local moneylenders, usually at exorbitant interest rates.

In an innovative approach to tackling this, IKEA has helped the women in these communities to form self-help groups. These women are encouraged to make small financial savings that they can later use to inter-loan within the community and reduce dependence on local moneylenders. These loans, with support from some nationalised banks, are then used to finance micro-enterprises that in turn help fund children's education.

IKEA's technical team did a study of local skills in the area and found the women to be extremely deft at embroidery. So, the company has now started directly placing orders for cushion covers with these women, without the interference of any middlemen. As a condition of sale, these women must be a part of the self-help community.

While IKEA tackles the issue in its supply chain with the help of UNICEF and local groups, members of the tobacco and chocolate industries are attempting to alleviate the problem collectively, with mixed results.

Tobacco Companies Tackle Child Labor

Global tobacco giants British American Tobacco [BAT], Philip Morris, Imperial Tobacco and Gallagher Group are members

Why Corporations Adopt Codes of Conduct

United States corporations have adopted corporate codes of conduct for a variety of reasons, ranging from a sense of social responsibility to pressure from competitors, labor unions, the media, consumer groups, shareholders and worker-rights advocates. The U.S. government has also encouraged U.S. corporations to adopt model business principles for their overseas operations.

Companies that import products from countries whose labor conditions have received negative publicity regarding child labor or abusive working conditions may develop codes of conduct in order to prevent further criticism. A Hong Kong trade lawyer stated in a recent article that many importers "just think it's wrong to have their goods made under conditions considered offensive. Others ... don't want to be exposed on *60 Minutes* or *20/20*."

Companies who spend hundreds of millions of dollars on advertising and whose sales depend heavily on brand image and consumer goodwill are particularly responsive to allegations that their operations exploit children or violate other labor standards. Some have cited positive correlations between responsible business behavior and return-on-investment, stock price, consumer preferences and employee loyalty. The CEO of Levi Strauss & Co. has said:

I believe—and our company's experience demonstrates—that a company cannot sustain success unless it develops ways to anticipate and address ethical issues as they arise. Doing the right thing from day one helps avoid future setbacks and regrets. Addressing ethical dilemmas when they arise may save your business from serious financial or reputational harm.

U.S. Department of Labor,
"Codes of Conduct in the U.S. Apparel Industry," www.dol.gov.

of the Eliminating Child Labour in Tobacco-Growing Foundation (ECLT), established in 2001, with the help of the ILO and the International Tobacco Growers' Association.

As most tobacco farms are family run, children working on them are not bonded labourers. The first challenge the ECLT Foundation faced was one of awareness raising among the farmers about the need for educating their children.

Following this, the partnership has been involved in building schools and digging wells for farmers in countries including Malawi, Uganda and Tanzania. In a recent move, it has also announced the decision to extend micro-credit to tobacco farmers in Kyrgyzstan at low interest rates. This aims to ensure that some farmers are able to send their children to school rather than keep them on the farms.

The foundation says it is "engaged in dialogue" with local governments and NGOs in order to "enlist their support" towards addressing the problem. It has established partners on the ground, it says, to monitor the progress on the various initiatives it funds.

But of the tobacco companies involved in this initiative, only BAT reports on the progress of the foundation's work (at some length) in its annual corporate responsibility report. BAT makes detailed references to commitments towards addressing the problem of child labour in tobacco growing, while the other companies are reticent, publishing little information on targets and real achievements.

Out of the eight ECLT projects currently underway in various countries, BAT has directly run four of these—in Brazil, Mexico, Fiji and Pakistan. Under the programmes run in Brazil, BAT subsidiary Souza Cruz subcontracts to farmers with children only if they produce a declaration of school attendance signed by a teacher or headmaster. Breach of the condition ends the contract.

The Role of Lobbying

Peter McAllister, executive director of the International Cocoa Initiative funded by chocolate industry members such as Hershey, Mars, Cadbury Schweppes and Nestlé and aimed at tackling child labour, says businesses should engage with governments on the issue. He says companies have an imperative to engage governments if they are not implementing national laws and international conventions on child labour that they have ratified.

McAllister says companies should identify influential NGOs and advocacy groups that could initiate conversations with governments to convince them of the risks of the child labour problem—the risks of business boycotts and the loss of an educated workforce.

He says companies have a range of tools, including staff training resources, database designing capabilities and policy framing skills, that they can offer to governments.

While the support programmes to eradicate child labour are ongoing in the cocoa farms of West Africa, industry-led certification systems that would measure progress and declare farms child-labour-free were not in place by the agreed date of 1 July 2005.

Business clearly has its own important role to play in finding creative solutions to the problem of child labour.

Businesses Must Find Creative Solutions

Jeroo Master, a child protection officer at UNICEF India, says that if governments were approached through intermediaries such as UNICEF or the ILO, officials may be less prone to hostility towards business's suggestions. Master sees the corporate role as "helping with the capacity-building of government law enforcement mechanisms".

While the biggest barrier to eliminating child labour remains the enforcement of national labour laws, international trade rules are beginning to factor in the issue of child labour.

Recently the European Parliament called on the European Commission to bring legal action against any European importers found using child labour. Members of the European Parliament also want the commission to make compliance with labour standards, including child labour norms, a condition in its own purchasing and contracting policies. MEPs want the commission to make tackling child labour a permanent element of bilateral trade deals with developing nations.

While the governments of the EU [European Union] and the US [United States] are looking at ways to tackle the issue via trade rules and political pressure, business clearly has its own important role to play in finding creative solutions to the problem of child labour.

Ireland Must Join the Fight Against Child Labor

Justin Kilcullen

According to Justin Kilcullen, recent organizational campaigns in Ireland against child labor have been prominent and have generated much interest. Child labor ruthlessly exploits young people, and it must be ended. However, Ireland's government has not been actively involved in world efforts to abolish child labor, and it must take steps to aid in the global fight. Particularly, Kilcullen declares, Ireland should become a donor nation to IPEC, the International Programme on the Elimination of Child Labour. Justin Kilcullen is director of the Irish organization Trócaire, which means mercy and compassion in Gaelic. Trócaire works toward "a just world where people's dignity is ensured, the rights of individuals are respected and where basic needs are met."

As you read, consider the following questions:

1. According to Kilcullen, what are the primary causes of child labor?
2. What is IPEC doing to combat child labor?
3. What four things does Kilcullen suggest Ireland should do to fight child labor?

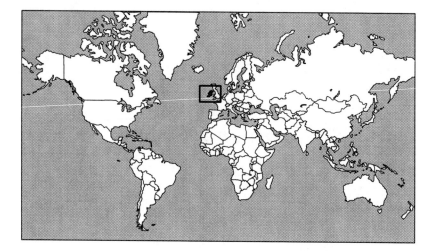

You may have seen Trócaire's [a human rights organization in Dublin] Lenten [referring to the Catholic season of Lent] campaign advertisement on TV or in the cinema in recent weeks [Spring 2006]. The campaign theme this year is child labour. Ireland must join the international programme to eliminate child labour. . . .

The advertisement depicts a job interview between a coffee plantation owner in Nicaragua and a child. All of the conditions outlined in the advertisement are true—punishing long hours, hazardous working conditions, little pay, no support in case of illness or injury. The only slightly misleading feature is the scenario being depicted. No child would ever be granted the courtesy of having the appalling conditions in which she or he will work explained to them.

Child labour is about ruthless exploitation of young lives.

Ruthless Exploitation

Child labour is about ruthless exploitation of young lives. Most thus exploited are condemned to a life of unceasing poverty and probably an early grave.

Not since Trócaire ran its campaign on modern day slavery in 2001 has there been such a public response to a Lenten campaign. It is interesting how the two issues are so closely linked.

Bonded labour, the modern form of slavery, also involves the exploitation of children. All told, the International Labour Organisation (ILO) estimates that more than 180 million children worldwide are caught up in unacceptable forms of child labour; that is one in six of the world's children.

While children have long been doing work the world over, and have made a positive contribution to domestic and even national income, the ILO distinguishes between this form of work and child labour which exposes children to harm or exploitation.

It includes hazardous work, such as that carried out by children in many coffee plantations in Nicaragua today, forced labour and labour performed by a child under a specified age for such work (e.g. quarry work). Such work interferes with a child's education and thus prevents the individual from eventually escaping the poverty trap.

Other forms of child exploitation also threaten their wellbeing: prostitution, pornography, forced recruitment into armed forces and trafficking.

Causes of Child Labour

The primary cause of child labour in the developing world is poverty. Family poverty pushes children into the labour market to earn money to supplement the family income or even as a means of survival. The lack of education, high dependence on an agricultural economy as a whole as well as traditions and cultural expectations are among factors that play a role in the occurrence of child labour.

More recently, the increased numbers of child-headed households, primarily linked to HIV/AIDS and armed con-

Slow Progress in Ending Worldwide Child Labor

This table shows regional trends in children's work, 2000–2004 (5 to 14 year olds).

Region	Child population (million)		Economically active children (million)		Activity rate (%)	
	2000	2004	2000	2004	2000	2004
Asia and the Pacific	655.1	650.0	127.3	122.3	19.4	18.8
Latin America and the Caribbean	108.1	111.0	17.4	5.7	16.1	5.1
Sub-Saharan Africa	166.8	186.8	48.0	49.3	28.8	26.4
Other regions	269.3	258.8	18.3	13.4	6.8	5.2
World	1,199.3	1,206.6	211.0	190.7	17.6	15.8

TAKEN FROM: Frank Hagemann, Yacouba Diallo, Alex Etienne, and Farhad Mehran, Global Child Labour Trends: 2000 to 2004. Geneva International Labour Office, 2006.

flict, brings increased pressure on children to work. Policies to eliminate child labour must address the multidimensional nature of the problem.

Finding a Solution

What can Ireland do to play a greater role in eliminating this scandal from today's world?

The ILO is charged with implementing the international convention that outlaws child labour. It also assists countries in establishing programmes to eliminate this form of exploitation and supports programmes that help children to escape from their employers and go to school, enjoy their childhood and be prepared to lead a fulfilled adult life.

Ireland supports the work of the ILO. Indeed, following Trócaire's campaign on slavery and in response to public support for this, the government undertook to support the organisation's work in countering bonded labour.

This year provides an opportunity for Ireland to make a further contribution to the work of the organisation. On May 4th [2007] the International Labour Organisation will publish a global report focusing specifically on how member states are working to tackle the problem through the International Programme to Eliminate Child Labour.

As yet Ireland does not support the IPEC. It is surely time to join the 30 donor countries that do so.

That programme, IPEC, has set out the measures that need to be taken to tackle this scourge—achieving universal primary education, improving the quality of education and teachers, income support to families to defray the losses of money when their children go back to school and implementing legislation that outlaws child labour.

As yet [in 2006] Ireland does not support the IPEC. It is surely time to join the 30 donor countries that do so. Such an action will fit very well into Ireland's current overseas development aid priorities.

Sub-Saharan Africa, where Irish Aid focuses its efforts, is a major problem area. Ireland's priority countries for development aid are all members of IPEC. Indeed Tanzania has undertaken a time-bound programme of action to implement IPEC. But there is still a shortage of donor funds to assist developing countries in achieving the standards set out in this programme.

Given the emphasis on education and poverty reduction, such support would be a natural extension of Ireland's current priorities.

In June [2006], the ILO will have its annual meeting. Between now and then Ireland should do a number of things:

- welcome the ILO's global report on child labour,

- indicate its intention to become a donor to IPEC;

- lobby those countries that have not yet done so to join the 87 others that have adopted IPEC, and

- become a passionate spokesperson in international forums such as the UN [United Nations], World Bank and EU [European Union] for the elimination of child labour.

Unless there is concerted action by wealthy governments, another generation of children will be condemned to a life of poverty.

Brazil Is Leading the Way Toward Eliminating Child Labor

International Labour Organization

In the following viewpoint, the International Labour Organization lauds Brazil for leading the fight against child labor as a result of its ability to identify child laborers and move them from the work environment to schools. A new initiative between Brazil and the International Labour Organization will use Brazilian know-how in the fight against global child labor. This "South-South" initiative, referring to cooperation among the nations in the Southern Hemisphere, will apply Brazil's strategies to other developing countries such as Haiti, Angola, and Mozambique in an effort to move more children from employment to education. The International Labour Organization (ILO) is an agency of the United Nations that deals with labor issues. It is located in Geneva, Switzerland.

As you read, consider the following questions:

1. What is the "Memorandum of Understanding" (MOU) between Brazil and the ILO designed to do?
2. Which countries in Africa and in the Caribbean will benefit from Brazil's know-how in combating child labor?

International Labour Organization, "Sharing Experience: A New Global Initiative Against Child Labour Goes from South to South," *World of Work*, vol. 62, April 2008, pp. 18–20. Reproduced by permission.

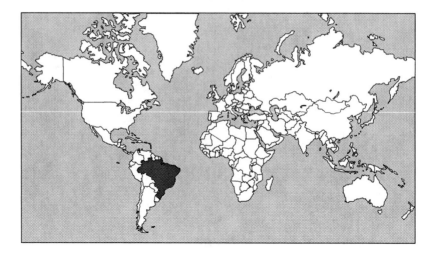

3. For what two reasons has Brazil become a reference point for fighting child labor?

In the increasingly successful global campaign against child labour, new lines of action are being drawn from "South to South".

Brazil, one of the countries with the most successful programme against child labour, has drawn up a new "South-South" charter in collaboration with the ILO [International Labour Organization] that will allow a sharing of experiences with other countries with similar goals.

Brazil has promoted South-South cooperation in other issues, but this is the first time the approach has been applied to fighting child labour.

"The diplomacy of the 21st century must be the diplomacy not only of interests but also of active solidarity, in a way that it reaches the people in other countries with concrete and continuous actions," says the Brazilian Minister of Foreign Affairs, Celso Amorim. He adds that a new agreement signed with the ILO will be essential to guaranteeing the sustainability of technical cooperation projects on the elimination of child labour.

A New Initiative

Last December [2007], Brazil and the ILO launched a new worldwide initiative to promote specific South-South technical cooperation projects and activities that contribute effectively to the prevention and elimination of child labour, particularly in its worst forms. The "Memorandum of Understanding [MOU] between the International Labour Organization and the Government of the Federative Republic of Brazil for the Establishment of the South-South Cooperation Initiative to Combat Child Labour" places Brazil and the ILO in the vanguard of the South-South cooperation, according to Mr. Amorim.

Brazil has promoted South-South cooperation in other issues, but this is the first time the approach has been applied to fighting child labour. The new initiative is designed to help other countries enhance their structure and coordination of their programmes against child labour. Among those countries are two Lusophone [Portuguese-speaking] countries in Africa, Angola and Mozambique, and Haiti in the Caribbean. The South-South cooperation initiative launched by Brazil is not only an opportunity for countries to benefit from the Brazilian experience in combatting child labour, but also for Brazil to learn from other countries in a spirit of horizontal cooperation. This is why the MOU includes not only countries that would "need" the technical assistance of Brazil, but countries such as India and South Africa, where a real partnership and an exchange of good practices in methodologies for combatting child labour can be undertaken.

Brazil as a Leader

Among developing or middle-income countries Brazil has become a reference point in the struggle against child labour for two reasons. Firstly, Brazil has had 15 years of experience in creating and implementing the technology needed to identify working children, take them out of exploitative work and get them into schools while providing their families with some income in what is known as "conditional cash transfer programmes". Secondly, Brazil has been strengthening its social dialogue structures based on sound civil society coordination to improve social control over public policies in a way that keeps alive consensus building and focus among employers, workers and the government on the issue.

The new agreement with the ILO sets out clear responsibilities for the Brazilian Cooperation Agency (ABC) and the Ministry of Foreign Affairs in furthering current efforts to assist other developing countries in the struggle against child labour while clearly defining the role of the ILO's International Programme on the Elimination of Child Labour (IPEC) and the ILO's office in Brazil.

"This is essential, as it stimulates the horizontal cooperation and sharing of good practices, and allows a better empowerment by developing countries, moving them into the driver's seat," says Michele Jankanish, Director of ILO/IPEC. "It corresponds to the spirit of Convention 182 on the Worst Forms of Child Labour regarding cooperation between nations."

She adds that the agreement "will also imply close links between colleagues in all countries, as more horizontal cooperation is expected."

For Lais Abramo, Director of the ILO Brazil Office, such horizontal cooperation is essential to promoting the cooperation and social dialogue needed to prevent and to eliminate child labour.

"With the Memorandum, we are inaugurating a new phase of dialogue for construction of criteria that, with no doubt, will strengthen the mission of the international cooperation of the ILO," she says.

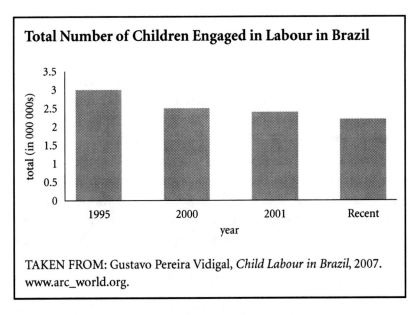

Total Number of Children Engaged in Labour in Brazil

TAKEN FROM: Gustavo Pereira Vidigal, *Child Labour in Brazil,* 2007. www.arc_world.org.

This translates into more effective projects on the ground. Maria Beatriz Cunha, Programme Officer of the ILO Brazil Office (and former IPEC CTA in Brazil), says the MOU "reaffirms the commitment and the policies for the application of the ILO Convention 138 on minimum age and Convention 182" and will bolster efforts by Brazil and its partners in civil society to share their experiences with other countries.

Expanding the Project

The project is also expected to extend to India, South Africa and some other members of Mercosur [a common market among several southern countries] to promote a dialogue on possible cooperation based on existing good practices. The ILO-Brazil initiative is also designed to create a forum for South-South cooperation in the fight against child labour among regional groups such as the Andean Pact, Mercosur, CPLP [Community of Portuguese Language Countries], and India-Brazil-South Africa Trilateral (IBSA) to foster horizontal cooperation among countries sharing successful experiences in the fight against child labour.

"The Memorandum aims to qualify the interchange of specialists and research, beyond the execution of projects of technical cooperation," says the director of ABC, ambassador Luiz Henrique Pereira da Fonseca, adding that ABC is ready to work with the ILO to coordinate the consolidation and systematization of Brazilian good practices in a manner appropriate to situations in other developing countries.

Angola and Mozambique have already undertaken projects that anticipated the new South-South contacts, and a new ABC-funded project has been announced on eliminating and preventing the worst forms of child labour in Haiti. Structured as a pilot project, the Haiti project aims to withdraw 200 children from the worst forms of child labour and get them into primary education. It also may prevent another 600 girls and boys at risk from being exploited at work. In addition, Guinea-Bissau has also announced its interest in hosting a project of this nature.

Such cooperation is vital, according to ILO experts, to strengthen efforts in some Portuguese-speaking countries where the number of child labourers hasn't declined as rapidly as in Latin America.

The Haiti project aims to withdraw 200 children from the worst forms of child labour and get them into primary education.

"The Memorandum of Understanding is a portrait of the experience that the ILO has been developing," says Pedro Oliveira, from IPEC Brazil. "It is a symbol of the philosophy of the ILO of continuously sharing experience, in the context of the United Nations and the world of work."

The Philippines Has Taken Measures to End the Worst Forms of Child Labor

Visayan Forum Foundation

According to Visayan Forum Foundation, the Philippines is systematically attacking its child labor problem through a coordinated effort by a number of organizations and local governments. These efforts target the worst forms of child labor as designated by the International Labour Organization (ILO) and aim to reduce these forms of labor significantly over the next decade. Stiff penalties are in place for those who employ child laborers, but the author points out that enforcement must follow in order for child labor laws to be effective. The fight against child labor in the Philippines is a difficult one, but anti-child labor organizations are continually learning enhanced strategies to deal with the problem. The Kasambahay Journal is the official publication of Visayan Forum Foundation, a Filipino nongovernmental agency that promotes social justice.

As you read, consider the following questions:

1. According to the author, what "two-pronged strategy" is the Philippines using to reduce child labor?
2. What role does the Visayan Forum Foundation play in attacking child labor?

Visayan Forum Foundation, "The End of Child Labor Within Reach," *Kasambahay Journal*, January–June 2006, pp. 4–6. Reproduced by permission.

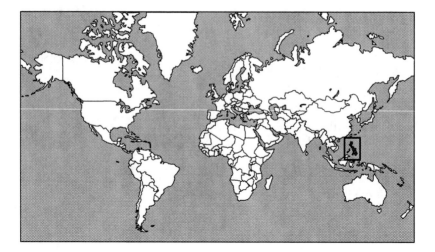

3. What two local governments in the Philippines have passed ordinances to register domestic workers?

If current trends continue, the worst forms of child labor can be eliminated worldwide within the next decade. A future where children are free from slavery, forced labor, trafficking, and hazardous or exploitative work may be within reach.

This positive outlook comes from the International Labour Organization's (ILO) recent global report which reveals that the past four years have seen an 11% decrease in child labor worldwide, with a 26% reduction in the number of children engaged in hazardous work.

ILO has urged all countries to commit themselves to the abolition of child labor in its worst forms by the year 2016, in line with sweeping national ratifications across the globe of ILO Convention No. 182, or the "Convention Concerning the Prohibition and Immediate Action for the Elimination of the Worst Forms of Child Labour."

The Philippines Has Been Proactive on Child Labor

To achieve this goal, ILO has urged countries to design and put in place by 2008 time-bound measures for the eradication of the worst forms of child labor—a step that has already been taken in the Philippines.

[In 2000], the Philippines ratified Convention 182. By June 28, 2002, it had become one of the first countries to launch a Time-Bound Program (TBP) for the elimination of the worst forms of child labor, a key program in support of the overarching National Program Against Child Labor (NPACL).

The NPACL is anchored on the vision of harnessing collective action of social partners to eliminate the worst forms of child labor and to transform the lives of child laborers, their families, and communities by enhancing their sense of self-worth, empowerment and development.

Social partners have targeted a 75% reduction in the number of children in the worst forms of child labor by the year 2015.

Social partners have targeted a 75% reduction in the number of children in the worst forms of child labor by the year 2015. Notably, based on consultations undertaken in preparation for the TBP, child domestic labor is included as one of six priority sectors of child labor to be targeted, along with sugarcane plantations, pyrotechnics, deep-sea fishing, mining and quarrying, and prostitution.

The US [United States] Department of Labor has supported ILO-International Programme on the Elimination of Child Labour (IPEC) Manila to implement a five-year support project which pursues a two-pronged strategy in tackling child labor. The two-pronged strategy follows from the need to simultaneously strengthen the "enabling" environment for the

229

elimination of the worst forms of child labor through such actions as awareness-raising and policy advocacy, while also engaging in direct interventions with vulnerable children, families, and communities.

ILO-IPEC Manila has been working with its local partners to educate the public about the worst forms of child labor; facilitate educational and economic opportunities for families identified as at risk of sending their children into child labor; build local capacity to detect, remove, and rehabilitate child laborers; and ensure that child labor-related concerns are mainstreamed into local and national policies.

Among its key partners is the Visayan Forum Foundation (VF) which works on child domestic work issues. As of June 2006, a two-year VF project within the Philippine Time-Bound Program (PTBP) framework has been completed. This action plan included activities to strengthen the capacity of local governments, employers' and workers' organizations, school and church groups, and children themselves to implement positive actions for child domestics.

The program also included policy advocacy, awareness-raising on good practices in addressing child domestic labor, and outreach and empowerment activities for child domestic laborers.

Removing Children from the Worst Forms of Child Labor

Former Labor and Employment Secretary Patricia Sto. Tomas reported that some 12,500 children have been removed from the worst forms of child labor and extended educational assistance under the PTBP as early as July of 2005.

These children were found working in pyrotechnics, prostitution, domestic labor, mining and quarrying, deep-sea fishing, and sugar cane plantations in Bulacan, Metro Manila, Iloilo, Camarines Norte, Negros Occidental, Oriental Negros, Cebu, and Davao.

The DOLE's Bureau of Women and Young Workers (BWYW) report also indicated that the children were among those identified through the baseline surveys conducted in 2003 and 2004 by IPEC through its local partners.

The BWYW report revealed that a total of 12,757 children were found engaged in the worst forms of child labor, of which over 12,300 children have been enrolled in formal education through a collaborative arrangement between the PTBP and World Vision, Plan International, ERDA, and the Christian Children's Fund.

Another 77 child laborers have been provided with non-formal education and 116 others with vocational skills training. Approximately 3,732 child workers enrolled in formal education have also been provided with school uniforms, books, school supplies, and financial support.

Sto. Tomas said the provision of educational and skills training assistance to the children is aimed at enabling them to engage in more productive economic activities than those that had subjected them to the worst forms of child labor.

"Education is the best form of intervention that would eliminate the worst forms of child labor," she said. "At the same time, livelihood assistance is extended to families of child workers to prevent their children from engaging again in the worst forms of child labor."

ILO-IPEC continues to support its partners in their efforts to combat child labor. Recently, for example, it released P7.1 million [Philippine pesos] to two of its non-government organization partners in Negros Oriental that are involved in the campaign to wipe out child labor.

Of the amount, P4.1 million will be given to the livelihood and education components of Goretti Foundation's Children at Risk and Children in Labor, to be used in its programs in Sta. Catalina, Siaton, Basay, Bais City, Mabinay, and Bayawan City.

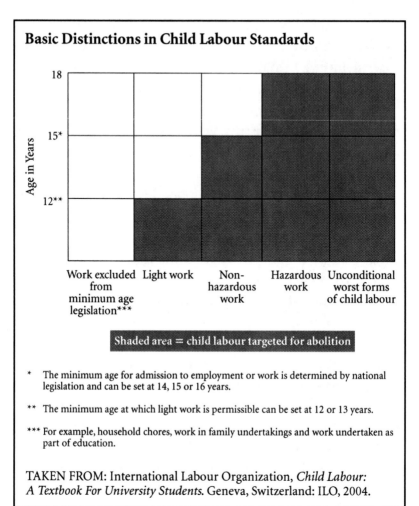

Basic Distinctions in Child Labour Standards

Age in Years: 18, 15*, 12**

Columns (left to right):
Work excluded from minimum age legislation*** — Light work — Non-hazardous work — Hazardous work — Unconditional worst forms of child labour

Shaded area = child labour targeted for abolition

* The minimum age for admission to employment or work is determined by national legislation and can be set at 14, 15 or 16 years.

** The minimum age at which light work is permissible can be set at 12 or 13 years.

*** For example, household chores, work in family undertakings and work undertaken as part of education.

TAKEN FROM: International Labour Organization, *Child Labour: A Textbook For University Students.* Geneva, Switzerland: ILO, 2004.

The remaining P3 million will go to the Association for the Welfare of Filipino Children for its school-based guidance counseling and tutorial program in Ayungon, Siaton, and Sibulan.

Enhanced Policies

Early on, a crucial development in the fight against child labor occurred during the TBP. The Philippines enacted RA 9231, or the Anti Child Labor Law of 2003, which reflects the principles of ILO Convention 182.

RA 9231 criminalizes and mandates stiff penalties (including fines of 100,000 to 1 million pesos and/or imprisonment for 12–20 years) for those who employ or facilitate the employment of children in the worst forms of child labor. To date, nobody has yet to be prosecuted under this new law.

A creative and proven way to increase public awareness about this law is to encourage TV producers to display a banner focusing on the importance of having secured a Working Child's Permit (WCP) "as [children's] employment in such public entertainment or information is essential."

RA 9231 [an anti-child labor law] criminalizes and mandates stiff penalties . . . for those who employ or facilitate the employment of children in the worst forms of child labor.

Child participation is also seen in action as working children have been given an increased role in the formulation of national policies such as the Medium-Term Philippine Development Plan and the Education for All National Action Plan.

Mainstreaming child labor concerns remains quite a challenge. However, some meaningful progress has been made on the level of local government. A few local governments specifically in Quezon City and Makati have passed local ordinances to provide for the large-scale registration of domestic workers within their jurisdictions.

Lessons

While it is still very early to assess the full impact of IPEC's support project, several important lessons are already emerging. The following insights stem from Visayan Forum's implementation of its action plan on child domestic labor, which has resulted in the withdrawal of more than 1,700 children from exploitative domestic work; the prevention of more than

1,300 other children from becoming domestics; and the return to formal schooling for many domestic workers.

First, more serious efforts must be made to popularize the provisions of the Anti Child Labor Law or RA 9231. This law has yet to gain any significant level of awareness among frontline law enforcers and labor inspectors. There are still many misconceptions about it stemming from a lack of appreciation about the debates of child labor. Implementation rules for this law need to be thoroughly discussed in consonance with recently enacted laws on trafficking and local policies for the registration of domestics. In the future, advocacy efforts should target the expansion of broad public support and clearly inform all actors of the role that they play.

Second, implementation of child labor programs requires effective functioning and coordination among different agencies. Without sufficient political will and financial commitment, new policies remain ineffective. For example, quick response teams cannot sustain removal and rescue of exploited children without the help of other institutions, mainly civil society groups, to provide shelter and re-integration services. Likewise, efforts to prevent children from entering the worst forms of child labor should be tied to access to quality education, which remains problematic.

Third, there is an urgent need to involve and build the capacity of local government actors (such as at the city and barangay [village] level) so that the provision of services and programs to child laborers will be sufficiently supported by existing local infrastructures. Without a strong sense of ownership, local agencies cannot be expected to embark on large-scale actions to eliminate the worst forms of child labor. Still, most local government units suffer from overstretched financial and human resources. In most cases, only one or two focal persons in a certain agency are tasked to monitor children, mobilize partners and deal with complaints from parents.

In a related manner, it is also desirable to establish a regular monitoring mechanism to track the increase or decrease of child labor in various areas of the Philippines; a proposal currently pending before national-level authorities could help to address this need, as it would allocate funding for a 5-yearly Survey on Children.

Working together to bring the dream of ending child labor within reach remains a continuing battle, and it will take all of our combined efforts to achieve victory.

Fortunately, the lessons learned over the past few years help to point the way into the future. Notably, as the fight against child labor moves forward, priority attention should be paid to increasing cooperation with and capacity-building of local actors including local government units, parents, communities, and of course children themselves.

Indeed, working together to bring the dream of ending child labor within reach remains a continuing battle, and it will take all of our combined efforts to achieve victory.

India Has Begun to Address the Complex Problem of Child Labor

Anupama Katakam

Anupama Katakam observes in the following viewpoint that in the Indian state of Maharashtra, thousands of children work in abysmal conditions, in violation of laws against such practices and threats of punishment for employers. Numerous raids have been conducted on sweatshops, but when authorities bring the children back home, their parents say that they cannot afford to raise them and that the children have been sent off to work in the hope of getting them a better life. Consequently, Katakam points out, many of these rescued children return to work, and the child labor industry continues through what is essentially a recycling of children. In 2005 the government of Maharashtra set up a child labor task force; together with non-governmental organizations, the government has begun to address the complex issue of child labor. Anupama Katakam is a journalist who writes for India's Frontline *magazine.*

As you read, consider the following questions:

1. To find a "zari factory," what signs does Katakam say a searcher should seek?

Anupama Katakam, "Young Slaves of Mumbai: Maharashtra Is Officially Child Labour-Free but the Exploitation of Children Continues in the Zari Units in Its Capital," *Frontline Magazine* (Madras, India), vol. 23, no. 6, April 7, 2006, p. 84. Reproduced by permission.

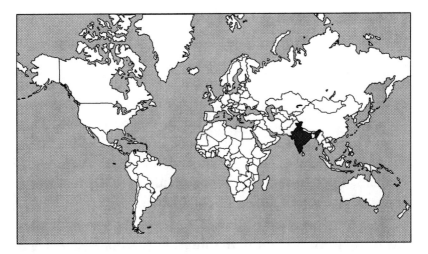

2. According to Katakam, how do "middlemen" prey on poor families?

3. According to the author, why is the penalty for employing children not a deterrent?

Walking through the lanes of Govandi [a suburb of Mumbai, formerly known as Bombay], past shanty-type structures, open sewers and garbage-filled passages is like going through any of Mumbai's sprawling slums. Unless you know what to look for, nothing would suggest that this slum, located in one of India's most progressive cities, harbours perhaps the worst form of human exploitation—bonded child labour.

Bits of fabric, gold threads, glitter beads and tiny fake pearls are some signs that invariably guide you to the dens of misery called "zari factories". Steep staircases lead to a trapdoor, which open into hovel-like rooms that house the zari units. Until recently, boys between the ages of six and 14 were found kneeling at low work tables sewing beads and coloured threads on to vast lengths of fabric. There are thousands of these factories in Mumbai spread across not just Govandi but other slums such as Dharavi and Madanpura.

Miserable Working Conditions

The boys work 20-hour days, seven days a week, in dingy 10' x 10' sized rooms. The rooms have hardly any ventilation and the floors are grimy. Each room has a small smelly bathroom located in one corner. Another corner serves as a basic cooking area. They sleep, bathe and eat in this same room. They are given two meals a day and, if lucky, two cups of tea. "It's a life of wretchedness," says Satish Kasbe, a social worker with Pratham, a non-governmental organisation (NGO) that works in rescue and rehabilitation of child labour.

The boys are rarely allowed to leave the room. If they must, they do so with an older boy who is a *karigar* (craftsman). And if they are lucky, the owner takes them on an occasional Sunday outing. Sometimes the owner locks the trapdoor, to open it only the next morning. Some rooms have two trapdoors. So if there is a raid, the children are shunted down the other one, which is then covered with a workbench.

The boys work 20-hour days, seven days a week, in dingy 10' x 10' sized rooms.

Child Abuse

Zari workers are split into *shagirds* (apprentices), *karigars* and owners. Most of the young boys are *shagirds*. In addition to doing some basic embroidery, a *shagird* does the cleaning and washing of clothes and some cooking for the unit. For this he is paid about Rs.50 [rupees] a month. Eventually he becomes a *karigar*. Physical and sexual abuse is part of this sad existence. In April 2005, 12-year-old Afzal Ansari, who worked in a unit in Govandi, died after contracting hepatitis. When Ansari fell ill, his employer did not treat him. Instead he asked a relative to take the boy away. Ansari died on the way to hospital. A post-mortem revealed marks left by burning cigarettes all over the boy's body and several signs of sexual abuse.

In June 2005, 11-year-old Ahmed Khan, another zari worker in Govandi, died after being beaten severely. According to his co-workers, the employer made the little boy massage his feet every evening. Khan did not do a very good job one day and the employer began thrashing him. Among other forms of torture, he pulled out the boy's fingernails.

Data collected from the State Labour Department say 90 per cent of children in the zari units in Mumbai are migrants from Uttar Pradesh and Bihar. They come from very poor districts such as Rampur and Azamgarh in Uttar Pradesh and Madhubani and Sitamarhi in Bihar. West Bengal, Jharkhand, Chhattisgarh and Andhra Pradesh are some of the other States from where children are brought.

Kasbe, who has rescued and taken several children back to their families, says the areas they come from are extremely backward. There are no schools in the villages or even close by. Most families are landless and work for a daily wage—that is if they can find work. "It could be as little as Rs.10–20 a day," he says. Some have land but suffer through drought or other calamities and therefore have no resources to bring up children. In several cases, he says, one parent has died so the ablest child is sent to work to support the family.

Desperate Families Send Their Children to Work

"When we return the kids, we ask the parents why they sent them," says Kasbe. Many say they cannot afford to look after them. Some believe that by sending the children they save them from a miserable life in the village. Those who live in border areas say sending children to Mumbai prevents them from joining terrorist or naxalite [Communist] outfits. In Mumbai, they believe the child will get at least an education and the opportunity of a better existence.

Zari owner Shankar Jha used to employ 15 children in his unit. "Their parents send them knowing full-well what the children will be doing. They are very poor and this fetches them some money and saves them from things such as bonded labour," he said. As to why they are kept like bonded labour, he says: "We try to do the best for the boys but our margins are so low that we can only spend a small amount on their well-being."

"When we return the kids, we ask the parents why they sent them," says [social worker Satish] Kasbe. "Many say they cannot afford to look after them."

Middlemen, says Kasbe, prey on these families. They go to vulnerable areas and convince families to send children to Mumbai by promising them an education. Some talk to children directly and lure them to big cities promising a better life. Others just kidnap them, he says.

Twelve-year-old Umesh Paswan, rescued recently from a zari factory in Govandi, says he came to Mumbai from Sita-marhi after an uncle promised to send him to school. His mother had died and his father had abandoned him. Paswan had nowhere to go. Mumbai seemed a good option. "I used to work from 5 a.m. to midnight. My eyes would water and my back and legs would hurt all the time. If the work was not good, I would get beaten."

It took the tragic deaths of [two child laborers], reported widely in the media, for the State government to initiate some action to rescue the thousands of children working in completely inhuman conditions.

Tackling the Child Labor Problem

Activists and social workers have been fighting a long battle to get the Maharashtra [a state in Western India] government to tackle the problem. "It seemed like the number of children working in these factories kept increasing," says Bhavana Kamble, a social worker in Govandi and Dharavi. "Either they are wearing blinkers or they do not think it's a big enough problem."

It took the tragic deaths of Khan and Ansari, reported widely in the media, for the State government to initiate some action to rescue the thousands of children working in completely inhuman conditions.

Immediately after the boys' deaths, 400 children were rescued in a dramatic raid in the Madanpura area, which has perhaps the highest number of zari factories in Mumbai. In the following months, about 16,000 children were rescued and sent back to their villages. Another 1,080 were rehabilitated in shelters. The Labour Department says there must be at least another 25,000 children working in this sector, whom it plans to rescue.

Towards the end of 2005, the State government set up a Special Child Labour Task Force. In February 2006 Deputy Chief Minister R.R. Patil declared that Maharashtra would be "child labour free" by August 15—an ambitious goal given the complexities of the problem but nonetheless a move in the right direction. Furthermore, Patil announced that employing children would be made a non-bailable offence in the State.

Recycling the Child Laborers

While a task force may solve the immediate problem, the child labour situation in Mumbai is so grim that the greater issue that needs addressing is why these children come here and what happens to them once rescued, says Ashok Agarwal, lawyer and civil rights activist. With no long-term rehabilitation plan, many of the children "saved" return to these sweatshops. "This is nothing but recycling of child labour," says Agarwal.

According to the Central Labour Department, India has about 10 crore [1 crore = 10 million] children in the workforce. Maharashtra comes eighth among the top 10 States that

An Organization Rescues Child Workers

Rambho Kumar was rescued from a carpet loom in India where he was forced to work 19 hours a day with no pay. The loom owner and trafficker seduced Rambho's mother with promises that Rambho would go to school and send money home to the family. Rambho's father had just died and his mother could not feed the family. She sent Rambho with the trafficker.

When Rambho's fingers bled from overwork the slave owner would dip them in oil and light a match to them. He wasn't allowed to play or go to school. He was never allowed to visit his family or leave the loom.

Finally, Rambho was rescued by liberators that [the organization] Free the Slaves works with on the ground. Today Ramhbo is free and he plans to help his mother find a house. He also wants to make sure no other children become enslaved.

Free the Slaves, "In Their Own Words: Rambho Kumar," www.freetheslaves.net.

employ child labour on a large scale. Why the government has suddenly become proactive in an area that has been screaming for attention for so many years is unclear. None of the officers *Frontline* spoke to would comment directly on this. Additional Labour Commissioner P.T. Jagtap came closest to answering, saying that child labour is a responsibility spread across many departments. Since there was little coordination between them the issue slipped through the cracks.

"The task force has solved this problem. It makes us work together," he says. "Before the task force came we did not have the authority to arrest anyone who employed children. If a rescue operation had to be carried out we needed the cooperation of the police and the Municipal Corporation," says Jagtap. Chaired by the Labour Commissioner, the task force comprises representatives from the Finance, Education, Women and Child Welfare and Home Departments as well as from the police, the Municipal Corporation and NGOs.

"Our aim is to conduct mass raids, which involve 50–60 officers who target an area and begin a 'combing operation'. If we raid one owner, the others get to know very fast and chase the children to hideaways. We need to go in there and attack as many factories as possible in one go," says Jagtap. The children that are rescued are taken to the Child Welfare Committee (CWC), which takes them home. Those who have nowhere to go would be given shelter. Currently they are kept in an observation home. But they are not delinquents, so they should not stay there. The Chief Minister has promised to set up residential schools for these children, says Jagtap.

Ineffective Laws and Punishments

"If there is political will, it is much easier to eradicate child labour," says Farida Lambay, Vice-Principal of the Nirmala Niketan College of Social Work. "It's not just about rescuing children, we need to tackle the problem at its shores." Compulsory education that is accessible to all is what we must work on, she says.

Gaps in legislation are the prime cause for the increasing rate of child labour, says Ashok Agarwal. The Child Labour (Prohibition and Regulation) Act, 1986, prohibits the engagement of children in certain employments (such as hazardous industries) and regulates the working conditions of children in certain other jobs. "The important thing is that the Act does not prohibit child labour in all its forms, nor does it lay down any provision for educational opportunities for rescued child labour." Agarwal has filed a public interest petition in the Supreme Court seeking the abolition of child labour in all forms and compulsory education for every child between six and 14 years, which is mandated by Article 21-A of the Constitution.

Furthermore, the penalty for employing children is so low that it is hardly a deterrent. The law says those caught employing children will pay fines between Rs.10,000 and Rs.20,000 or serve imprisonment from two to five years.

Additionally, says Agarwal, none of the other laws which protect children, such as the Juvenile Justice (Care and Protection of Children) Act, 2000; the Bonded Labour System (Abolition) Act, 1976; the Beedi and Cigar Workers (Conditions of Employment Act), 1966; and the Factories Act, 1948, provide for any form of rehabilitation for rescued children. In fact, laws are so skewed that the Apprentice Act, 1961, and the Plantation Labour Act, 1951, actually permit children to work. "If the lawmakers have decided to eradicate child labour, they must first make the laws cohesive," says Agarwal.

If working at the age of six to earn Rs.50 [rupees] a month is a better life, then clearly India has a long way to go.

There are two schools of thought when it comes to children working. One believes that as long as children are first educated, it is all right for them to work for the rest of the day. This would provide a poor family with some income. The other school seeks a blanket ban on children working. Unfortunately, activists and lawmakers seem stuck in this argument; as a result children continue to lose out on their childhood.

If working at the age of six to earn Rs.50 [rupees] a month is a better life, then clearly India has a long way to go before it can claim to be an emerging economy that has become a favourite in the global market.

Periodical Bibliography

Rick Docksai   "India's Progress in Reducing Child Labor;
                        New Economy's Need for Skilled Labor Sends
                        India's Youth Back to School, " *The Futurist*,
                        July–August 2008.

Laurie Goering   "Ending Child Labor Tricky Job for India,"
                        Chicago Tribune, April 18, 2008.

Colin McMahon   "Shifting Kids from Work to School Is Paying
                        off in Developing Nations," *Chicago Tribune*.
                        July 5, 2007.

Sandra Morgan   "Canada's Help Needed to Stop Worldwide
                        Child Labour Abuse," *Canadian Speeches*,
                        March/April 2002, pp. 10–17.

One World South Asia   "Education Must to End Child Labor," June 12
                        2008. http://southasia.oneworld.net.

Cathryn J. Prince   "Ending Child Labor: Tall Task for Nations,"
                        Christian Science Monitor, June 19, 1996.

Natalie Redstone   "Protecting Children from Child Labour," *Sister
                        Namibia*, March 2008.

William M. Reilly   "Child Labor on Way Out?" UPI, May 4, 2006.

Michael G. Schechter   "Working to Eliminate Human Rights Abuses
and Michael Bockenek   of Children: A Cross-National Comparative
                        Study," *Human Rights Quarterly*, August 2008.

Robert Senser   "Don't Shop Till They Drop," *U.S. Catholic*,
                        April 2007, pp. 24–26.

Tim Walker   "Reclaiming Lives," *NEA Today*, November
                        2008, pp. 30–33.

For Further Discussion

Chapter 1

1. After reading the viewpoints in this chapter, how would you assess the worldwide child labor problem? Is it still a major issue in cultures worldwide, or is enough being done to combat child labor on a world scale?

2. From reading the viewpoints in this chapter, does child labor seem to be mostly a third world issue or do developed countries struggle with this as well?

3. Lissa Wyman argues that fine carpets cannot possibly be made by the unskilled hands of young children while the Anti-Slavery Society argues just the opposite, that in countries such as India and Pakistan, young children are employed making carpets. Which argument seems more convincing to you?

Chapter 2

1. Many governments and organizations believe that it is more important to end the worst forms of child labor than to attack all child labor. Do you agree that the worst forms should be addressed first or that these forms are an outgrowth of the general child labor issue and that all child labor should be targeted?

2. Can the worst forms of child labor be ended, or do you believe that these forms, however objectionable and awful, fill a need in the world and may never be fully eradicated?

Chapter 3

1. Some experts believe that only when a country gains enough wealth to not need child labor can such a country

effectively eliminate the practice. Do you agree that child labor is an unsolvable issue in poor nations and that it should be allowed until the people of a country no longer need to send their children to work to survive? Why or why not?

2. Radley Balko has argued that child labor is a necessary step in a country's progress toward national prosperity. Do you believe that it is worth the sacrifice of millions of children to achieve this goal or do you feel that such ends do not justify the means? Please explain your answer.

3. Several of the authors in this section argue that boycotting companies that use child labor is not an effective strategy because it will just push children into even worse jobs, especially prostitution. Do you think boycotts can be successful or do you agree that they don't work? Please explain your answer.

Chapter 4

1. From your readings in this chapter, which countries seem to be the most effective in ending child labor, and why? What methods of attacking child labor seem the most promising?

2. It is evident from the viewpoints in this chapter that governments alone cannot tackle the global child labor issue, and that non-governmental organizations (NGOs) such as the International Labour Organization and Human Rights Watch are integral partners in combating child labor. How effective do these NGOs seem to be?

Organizations to Contact

The editors have compiled the following list of organizations concerned with the issues debated in this book. The descriptions are derived from materials provided by the organizations. All have publications or information available for interested readers. The list was compiled on the date of publication of the present volume; the information provided here may change. Be aware that many organizations take several weeks or longer to respond to inquiries, so allow as much time as possible.

Child Rights Information Network (CRIN)
Child Rights Information Network (CRIN)
London EC1M 4AR United Kingdom
+44 20 7012 6866 • fax: +44 20 7012 6952
e-mail: info@crin.org
Web site: www.crin.org

Child Rights Information Network (CRIN) is a global network that coordinates and promotes information and action on child rights. CRIN seeks to place children's rights at the top of the global agenda by addressing root causes and promoting systematic change. It has a variety of publications on child abuse and child labor available on its Web site.

Child Workers in Asia (CWA)
PO Box 26, Srinakharinwirot Post Office
Bangkok 10117 Thailand
++662 662 3866-8 • fax: ++662 261 2339
e-mail: cwanet@csloxinfo.com
Web site: www.cwa.tnet.co.th

Child Workers in Asia (CWA) was established in 1985 as a support group for child laborers in Asia and for the nongovernmental organizations (NGOs) working with them. It facilitates the sharing of expertise and experiences between

NGOs, and strengthens their collaboration to respond jointly to the exploitation of working children in the region. The *CWA Newsletter* is one of the many publications available on its Web site.

Fisek Institute
Selanik Cad. 52/4 Kizilay, Ankara
Turkey
++ 90-312-4197811 • fax: ++ 90-312-4252801
Web site: www.fisek.org

The Fisek Institute is a non-governmental organization in the field of occupational health and safety at the national level. It aims to raise the consciousness of the public in order to remove the reasons forcing children to work; to eliminate the factors that are dangerous for child laborers' health and safety at work; and to ensure improvement of health, identity, and self-esteem of working children. Research, essays and maps are available on the institute's Web site.

Free the Children
PO Box 32099, Hartford, CT   06150
(416) 925-5894 • fax: (416) 925-8242
Web site: www.freethechildren.com

Free the Children is a worldwide network of children helping children through education, with more than 1 million youths involved in the organization's education and development programs in forty-five countries. Founded in 1995 by international child rights activist Craig Kielburger, the primary goals of the organization are to free children from poverty and exploitation, and to free young people from the notion that they are powerless to bring about positive change in the world. Through domestic empowerment programs and leadership training, Free the Children inspires young people to develop as socially conscious global citizens and become agents of change for their peers around the world. Brochures and reports are available for download at the Free the Children's Web site.

Global March Against Child Labor
PO Box 4479, Kalkaji, New Delhi 110019
  India
+91 11 4132 9025 • fax: +91 11 4053 2072
e-mail: info@globalmarch.org
Web site: www.globalmarch.org

Global March Against Child Labor is a worldwide movement to protect and promote the rights of all children. The organization is especially concerned with children's right to receive a free, meaningful education; to be free from economic exploitation; and from performing any work that is likely to be harmful to the child's physical, mental, spiritual, moral, or social development. Its publications include reviews of child labor in countries such as Costa Rica, Bangladesh, Chile, and Niger; these publications are available for download on Global March's Web site.

Human Rights Watch
350 Fifth Avenue, 34th floor, New York, NY 10118-3299
(212) 290-4700 • fax: (212) 736-1300
e-mail: hrwnyc@hrw.org
Web site: http://hrw.org

Human Rights Watch is an independent, non-governmental organization dedicated to protecting the human rights of people around the world. Human Rights Watch investigates and exposes human rights violations and holds abusers accountable. It also challenges governments and those who hold power to end abusive practices and respect international human rights law, and enlists the public and the international community to support the cause of human rights for all. Human Rights Watch publishes numerous studies on bonded child labor, child soldiers, child domestic workers, and child slaves. These studies are available on its Web site.

International Research on Working Children (IREWOC)
Cruquiusweg 68-70
  The Netherlands

+ 31 (0)20 4651763
e-mail: info@irewoc.nl
Web site: www.childlabour.net

The International Research on Working Children (IREWOC) was founded in the Netherlands in 1992 to generate more research on child labor. It is a professional organization that looks at the issue of child labor from the perspective of child rights and with a focus on the socio-cultural and economic environment. IREWOC has a variety of child labor publications available on its Web site.

International Center on Child Labor and Education (ICCLE)
888 Sixteenth Street NW, Washington, DC 20006
(202) 974-8124 • fax: (202) 974-8123
E-mail: sjoshi@iccle.org
Web site: www.iccle.org

The International Center on Child Labor and Education (ICCLE) is a nonprofit organization dedicated to mobilizing worldwide efforts to advance the rights of all children. ICCLE is especially concerned that children receive a free and meaningful education and that they are free from economic exploitation and any work that is hazardous, interferes with their education, or is harmful to their health or physical, mental, spiritual, moral or social development. The Center serves as the international advocacy office of the Global March Against Child Labor, a movement representing some 2,000 organizations in 140 countries intended to highlight child slavery and hazardous child labor. The ICCLE Web site has publications concerning global child labor, including child labor in South America, Africa, and Asia.

International Labour Organization (ILO)
4 route des Morillons, Geneva CH-1211
  Switzerland
+41 (0) 22 799 6111 • fax: +41 (0) 22 798 8685
e-mail: ilo@ilo.org
Web site: www.ilo.org

The International Labour Organization (ILO) is a United Nations agency that is devoted to advancing opportunities for women and men to obtain decent and productive work in conditions of freedom, equity, security, and human dignity. It aims to promote rights at work, to encourage decent employment opportunities, to enhance social protection, and to strengthen dialogue in handling work-related issues. The ILO publishes numerous publications about global labor and child labor, including the magazine *World of Work*. Many of these publications are available on its Web site.

RugMark
RugMark USA, Washington, DC   20009
(202) 234-9050 • fax: (202) 347-4885
Info@RugMark.org
http://www.rugmark.org

RugMark is an international nonprofit organization devoted to building schools, programs, and opportunities in order to end child labor in the handmade carpet industry in South Asia. RugMark randomly inspects the looms of companies that agree to employ adults only. Through independent certification and rigorous inspections, RugMark verifies that rugs are produced by child-labor free companies.

United Nations Children's Fund (UNICEF)
125 Maiden Lane, 11th Floor, New York, NY   10038
(212) 686-5522
e-mail: information@unicefusa.org
Web site: www.unicef.org

The United Nations Children's Fund (UNICEF) was created to advocate for the protection of children's rights, to help meet children's basic needs, and to expand children's opportunities to reach their full potential. UNICEF strives to establish children's rights as enduring ethical principles and international standards of behavior toward children. UNICEF offers numerous publications, including a yearly summary called "The State of the World's Children," on its Web site.

United States Department of Labor
200 Constitution Avenue NW, Washington, DC 20210
866-4-USA-DOL
Web site: www.dol.gov

The U.S. Department of Labor fosters and promotes the welfare of the job seekers, wage earners, and retirees of the United States by improving their working conditions, advancing their opportunities for profitable employment, protecting their retirement and health care benefits, helping employers find workers, strengthening free collective bargaining, and tracking changes in employment, prices, and other national economic measurements. In carrying out this mission, the Department administers a variety of federal labor laws, including those that guarantee workers' rights to safe and healthy working conditions; a minimum hourly wage and overtime pay; freedom from employment discrimination; unemployment insurance; and other income support. Numerous publications about child labor, and labor in general, are available at the Department of Labor's Web site.

Bibliography of Books

Loretta
Elizabeth Bass
Child Labor in Sub-Saharan Africa. Boulder, CO: Lynne Rienner Publishers, 2004.

David B. Batstone *Not for Sale: The Return of the Global Slave Trade—and How We Can Fight It.* New York: HarperSanFrancisco, 2007.

Jonathan
Blagbrough
They Respect Their Animals More: Voices of Child Domestic Workers. London: Anti-Slavery International, 2008.

Rachel Burr *Vietnam's Children in a Changing World.* New Brunswick, NJ: Rutgers University Press, 2006.

Holly Cullen *The Role of International Law in the Elimination of Child Labor.* Boston, MA: Martinus Nijhoff Publishers, 2007.

Alec Fyfe *The Worldwide Movement Against Child Labour: Progress and Future Directions.* Geneva: International Labour Office, 2007.

Kathlyn Gay *Child Labor: Global Crisis.* Brookfield, CT: Millbrook, 1998.

Beverly
Carolease Grier
Invisible Hands: Child Labor and the State in Colonial Zimbabwe. Portsmouth, NH: Heinemann, 2006.

Laura Pincus
Hartman, Denis
Gordon Arnold,
and Richard E.
Wokutch

*Rising Above Sweatshops: Innovative
Approaches to Global Labor Challenges.* Westport, CT: Praeger, 2003.

Gamini Herath
and Kishor
Sharma

Child Labour in South Asia. Alder-
shot, UK: Ashgate Publishing, 2007.

Hugh D.
Hindman

Child Labor: An American History.
Armonk, NY: M.E. Sharpe, 2002.

Sandy Hobbs, Jim
McKechnie, and
Michael Lavalette

*Child Labor: A World History Com-
panion.* Santa Barbara, CA: ABC-
CLIO, 1999.

International
Labour Office and
International
Programme on
the Elimination
of Child Labour

*IPEC Action Against Child Labour,
2006–2007: Progress and Future Priorities.* Geneva, Switzerland: International Labour Organization, 2008.

International
Programme on
the Elimination
of Child Labour

*Rooting Out Child Labour from Cocoa
Farms.* Geneva, Switzerland: International Labour Organization, 2007.

Anne Kielland
and Maurizia C.
Tovo

*Children at Work: Child Labor Prac-
tices in Africa.* Boulder, CO: Lynne
Rienner Publishers, 2006.

Juliane
Kippenberg

*Bottom of the Ladder: Exploitation
and Abuse of Girl Domestic Workers
in Guinea.* New York: Human Rights
Watch, 2007.

Marvin J. Levine	*Children for Hire: The Perils of Child Labor in the United States.* Westport, CT: Praeger, 2003.
Milton Meltzer	*Cheap Raw Material.* New York: Viking, 1994.
Jeylan T. Mortimer	*Working and Growing Up in America.* Cambridge, MA: Harvard University Press, 2003.
Peter F. Orazem, Guilherme Luís Sedlacek, and Zafiris Tzannatos	*Child Labor and Education in Latin America: An Economic Perspective.* New York: Palgrave Macmillan, 2009.
David L. Parker	*Before Their Time: The World of Child Labor.* New York: Quantuck Lane Press, 2007.
M.M. Rehman, Kanta Rehman, and S. Mehartaj Begum	*Child Labour & Child Rights: A Compendium.* New Delhi: Manak Publications, 2002.
Tapan Kumar Shandilya and Ahmad Khan Shakeel	*Child Labour: A Global Challenge.* New Delhi, India: Deep & Deep Publications, 2003.
Anna M. Troubnikoff	*Trafficking in Women and Children: Current Issues and Developments.* Hauppauge, NY: Nova Science Publishers, 2003.

John Ungerleider   *Challenging Child Labor: Education and Youth Action to Stop the Exploitation of Children.* Brattleboro, VT: School for International Training, 2004.

Aruna Vasudevan   *Commerce and Trade.* Danbury, CT: Grolier, 2004.

Myron Weiner,   *Born Unfree: Child Labour, Education,*
Neera Burra, and   *and the State in India.* New Delhi:
Asha Bajpai   Oxford University Press, 2006.

Burns H. Weston   *Child Labor and Human Rights: Making Children Matter.* Boulder, CO: Lynne Rienner Publishers, 2005.

William G.   *Child Labor in America: History,*
Whittaker   *Policy, and Legislative Issues.* New York: Novinka Books, 2004.

Thom   *Human Trafficking.* Yankton, SD:
Winckelmann   Erickson Press, 2009.

Index

Geographic headings and page numbers in **boldface** refer to viewpoints about that country or region.